Advance Praise for *Power*

"In *Power*, Charity C. Elder provides a captivating case for the dopeness of Black women. Daring to reconsider past and contemporary realities beyond the gaze of oppression, Power uses soul stirring narratives and empirical data to illuminate our historical rise and shares fresh theories for how Black women manage to thrive in a twenty-first century context."

—**Timeka N. Tounsel**, author of *Branding Black Womanhood: Media Citizenship from Black Power to Black Girl Magic*

"*Power* explores the sociological evolution of understanding the development and expansion of Black women's acquisition of agency in America. Charity C. Elder's award-winning background prepared her to masterfully encapsulate the intersectional nuances of research and introspective analysis to interact with a diverse palate of readers. Elder births a new definition of 'Dopeness' to transform the historical association of Black women 'lacking' to create a new-aged literary presentation of Black women's 'pearls.' Power delivers Black women a new way to ruminate their position in society and unapologetically explore avenues toward purpose and success, demonstrating why black women truly do lead."

—**Glynda C. Carr**, president & CEO, Higher Heights for America

"*Power* is the right book, with the right message, for right now. It is an important book that shatters stereotypes and proves for the first time just how far Black women have come. Beautifully written, *Power* is a story of resilience and hope. I recommend that every Black woman, all women of color, read this book."

—**Minda Harts**, Workplace & Equity consultant and bestselling author of *The Memo*

"*Power* is the bouquet of flowers Black women have long deserved—an acknowledgment of all we have overcome and all we have achieved in spite of unparalleled challenges. It never shies away from the reality of the hardships we continue to face today but it gives us a moment to exhale at last. To reflect. To heal. To put down the heavy load for a moment and stand back and look at the garden of our lives and celebrate the bounty. It made me feel seen, and I know so many of my fellow sisters will feel seen as well. Above all, it was a much needed and comforting reminder that there is so much hope for our futures and the futures of our daughters."

—**Mandi Woodruff-Santos**, award-winning cohost of *Brown Ambition* and founder of the MandiMoney Makers

"In this compelling debut, Elder pens a meditation that celebrates African descended women's everyday strength, resilience, and determination to succeed, along with their expressions of joy, love, and excellence in a world that isn't always just. Elder writes about the ways "Black women be knowing," which goes beyond the typical narrative of depravity wrought by white supremacy and reveals elements of truth-telling that happens at the nexus of Blackness and womanism. This book is a call-to-action for deeper conversations about where society can go and how we can get there when we stop oppressing and start protecting Black and Brown women."

—**Yndia Lorick-Wilmot**, sociologist and podcast host of *Talking Journeys of Belonging 2 Blackness*

POWER

THE RISE OF
BLACK WOMEN
IN AMERICA

POWER

THE RISE OF
BLACK WOMEN
IN AMERICA

CHARITY C. ELDER

Skyhorse Publishing

Skyhorse Publishing books may be purchased in bulk at special discounts for sales promotion, corporate gifts, fund-raising, or educational purposes. Special editions can also be created to specifications. For details, contact the Special Sales Department, Skyhorse Publishing, 307 West 36th Street, 11th Floor, New York, NY 10018 or info@skyhorsepublishing.com.

Skyhorse® and Skyhorse Publishing® are registered trademarks of Skyhorse Publishing, Inc.®, a Delaware corporation.

Visit our website at www.skyhorsepublishing.com.

10 9 8 7 6 5 4 3 2 1

Library of Congress Cataloging-in-Publication Data is available on file.

Cover design by Kai Texel
Cover art © Carol Muthiga-Oyekunle/Lolita Lorenzo Art
Author photo by Hannah Forero

Permission to use "How I Got Over" lyrics granted by Clara and Willa Ward Publications and Estate of Jay B. Ross

Print ISBN: 978-1-5107-7002-7
Ebook ISBN: 978-1-5107-7084-3

Printed in the United States of America

To the Black women who taught me about sisterhood . . .

rebecca chaundreia elder
my big sister
a dope black woman

donalyn elnora elder
my baby sister
poet, writer & consummate advocate for the underdog
(1979–2006)

I am the dream and the hope of the slave.
I rise
I rise
I rise.

—Still I Rise | Maya Angelou, 1978

The new dawn balloons as we free it. For there is always light, if only we're brave enough to see it. If only we're brave enough to be it.

—The Hill We Climb | Amanda Gorman, 2021

we are the ones we have been waiting for

—Poem for South African Women | June Jordan, 1978

CONTENTS

PREFACE
A BLACK WOMAN'S GAZE

"This is the best time in America to be a Black woman."

I was in conversation with a former *Newsweek* editor; a white man in middle-age. By the look on his face, I could see that my words shocked him. I saw the puzzlement, incredulity. He said he was surprised. But his eyes seemed to go further, to say what his mouth did not: How can you or *any* Black woman be so confident and self-assured at this time?

It was late November 2016. Donald J. Trump was president-elect of the United States.

Half the country was inconsolable. The other half ebullient. At the time, I was an executive producer attending an after-work event on the rooftop of a Manhattan hotel, hobnobbing with compatriots in the business of reporting.

The city's lights shone brightly against the blue-black sky. But Manhattan, with its large democratic base, was shrouded in a thick, invisible funk. The 2016 presidential election season had been onerous; marked by white nationalism, misogyny, xenophobia, and high rates of police officers killing and brutalizing Black people.

I don't recall exactly what the journalist said to prompt my declaration, but I distinctly remember an urge to give voice. To center my narrative. To articulate my Black woman's gaze.

Black women are dope: dope as an adjective, not as a noun or verb; dope in Black urban parlance. During the late 1980s and early 1990s, in inner cities from Los Angeles to the Bronx, the definition of dope expanded from being synonymous with illicit drugs to being an adjective describing something or someone to be emulated, admired, and even envied.

Dope*ness* is not akin to "Black Girls Rock" or "Black Girl Magic," which are terms that have become so ubiquitous they've lost real meaning. Dope*ness* is not a catchphrase to be memed on Twitter, tatted on a forearm, or spray painted on a city block. Nor is it synonymatic with "Strong Black Woman," a toxic trope that dehumanizes and reduces Black women to workhorses and fixers absent of humanity, fragility, or vulnerability.

Centuries of oppression and abuse juxtaposed against collective rising is at the epicenter of this dope*ness*. It is not reserved for the "worthy" few. Dope*ness* is a prescription for Black women collectively. It is for any person who identifies as a Black woman, whether they live in anonymity caring for their families and communities or they've amassed great wealth and influence.

"This is the best time in America to be a Black woman." I understand the historical and institutional framework that underpinned the editor's reaction to my gaze. Still, I took umbrage at his inability to accept that I am proud to be a Black woman, regardless of the state of the nation.

Following that encounter, I performed a Google search using the key words "Black women" and "African American women." Curious, I wanted to understand the delta between my gaze and the veteran editor's perception. And while an internet search lacks scholarly rigor, the results were informative.

After reading news articles, academic surveys, and government studies about Black women, the consistent theme was LACK. Irrespective of the source, Black women were characterized by a lack of wealth, jobs, education, opportunity, resources, housing, health, beauty, mates, and so on. The themes and messages were painfully familiar. Centuries of oppression whispered to me, *Black women ain't shit, ain't got shit, never gon' be shit.* And as I stared at the search results displayed on the screen, I thought about my life: the failures and triumphs.

I remembered my mother's mantra, "You are special." I recalled my maternal and paternal grandmothers and their unspoken, yet lived lessons of dignity, excellence, pride, and self-respect. I reminisced about my dope sisters, aunties, cousins, and friends, so stylish, cool, and confident. I considered the Black women educators and those from church and work who'd shepherded and guided me. These dope Black women modeled ingenuity, gumption, and fortitude.

I had no interest in explaining to the former *Newsweek* editor why I believed in Black women; why I believed in myself. In the New Testament, Jesus said, "do not throw your pearls before pigs, for they will trample them under their feet and turn and tear you to pieces."[1] Trying to get him to understand "my pearls" would ultimately work against me. I've learned that it is better to focus on doing what needs to be done to advance, to move forward, to create a life I want to live.

The serendipitous conversation with the editor and the results of the Google search led to this book. I am determined to write what I know to be true about Black women, but more importantly to support my knowing with data and facts.

Black women are dope because they rise and are yet rising. This dopeness is not hyperbolic or symbolic—rather, it is borne of persecution that has failed to frustrate a perseverant persistence to prevail.

I wrote this book for Black women, particularly younger generations, and those yet to come. I intentionally share stories and data of triumph to inspire Black women to discover and pursue their own unique purpose in life. My greatest hope is that this book encourages Black women and propels them forward.

—*Charity C. Elder* | June 2022

CHAPTER 1

ACTS OF RESISTANCE

My mother was and is my first love. In my earliest memories, she is there. As a child, I often climbed into her bed at night and asked, "Can you tell me the story?" Holding me tightly against her bosom, lovingly caressing my face, I'd hear the story of my birth one more time.

I have childhood memories that are not as endearing. Even now, I wince in pain whenever I think of sitting on a stool between my mother's legs as she brushed, combed, and willed my curly coils into submission. And if I happened to move ever so slightly, I'd feel the sting of the brush on my head. And my mom would say, in a perfectly timed staccato: "Now. I. Said. Be. Still!" In the end, my mother always triumphed, styling my hair to her satisfaction; color-coordinated barrettes and ribbons la pièce de résistance.

I think fondly of those early years. And while I am not a mother, I can appreciate the effort my mom invested to make sure my sisters and I always looked, as she would say, "like somebody loved us." And her work did not go unnoticed. It was commonplace to receive compliments, at church, school, or the grocery store, about how cute we were or how well we were dressed. My mom reveled in the praise, and even as a little girl, I did too. But my mother's focus and efforts went well beyond grooming; she was intentional about shaping the adults we would become.

My mother was born in Connecticut in 1952, a couple of years before the landmark US Supreme Court decision *Brown v. Board of Education* effectively ended legal segregation in public schools. As a teenager, she witnessed the racial movements of the 1960s and the signing of the Civil Rights and the Voting Rights Acts into law.

The impact of being raised during the Civil Rights era, coupled with a strong faith, led my mother to instill values and a sense of worth in her three daughters. She taught us that we were special, beautiful, loved, and what other people thought about us was irrelevant. I'll never forget the lesson in snow. "Did you know that no two snowflakes are the same?" she would ask, "God made every snowflake special. And you're just like a snowflake; there is no one else like you in the whole world." My formative years cemented an understanding that I was priceless. I understood that I did not have to earn love; I had value because I am.

The love I received from Black women growing up extended beyond my mother. My childhood was buttressed by the love of my grandmothers, aunts, sisters, church sisters, teachers, and friends. The love I experienced, while unique *for me*, is not unique *to me*. It is not new, the Black women's praxis of instilling a strong sense of self in Black girls. It is a strategy, a form of resistance against oppression Black mothers have harnessed to insulate and protect their daughters for centuries. It should be noted that Black women resist in varied, innovative ways on behalf of their sons too, but I center my analysis on how they mother their daughters.

Like my mother, it can be argued that all (or nearly all) mothers endeavor to protect their children and to teach them the skills needed to survive and thrive. But for Black women, mothering is also an act of resistance. Rooted in slavery, passed down from mother to daughter for generations.

Before the birth of this nation, the codification and monetization of enslaved women expanded beyond free labor to the exploitation of their bodies and offspring. In 1662, Virginia's colonial government passed a law equating Black womanhood with slavery. Progeny of a Black woman, irrespective of paternity, was doomed to a lifetime of enslavement. In resistance, some enslaved women "did not bear offspring for the system at all. They used contraceptives and abortives in an attempt to resist the system, and to gain control of their bodies."[1] Every era since then has necessitated the creation and implementation of new tactics of resistance.

The legacy of Black mothers teaching their daughters to love, value, and respect themselves is not only a form of resistance against systems of oppression, but it has also developed into an ethos where Black women love, value, and respect Black women writ large. This regard has engendered a familiarity and connection—a knowing betwixt Black women.

Black women have an inner knowing of Black women. As a collective, in aggregate. A soul knowing that intuits dope*ness*. A knowing that honors shades of skin, textures of hair, curves of the body. A knowing that accepts imperfections and acknowledges humanity.

As Black women navigate the world, this inner knowing often reveals itself in an acknowledgment—from kin, friend, or stranger—by other Black women. It's a nonverbal, "I see you girl!" or the look exchanged between two Black women whenever someone does something crazy in public. When Black women see one another, they remember the Black women who taught them to value and love themselves, enabling them to value and love Black women.

Recently, I spent a few weeks visiting friends who live in a very small, very white hamlet north of New York City. Since I needed to run an errand, I went to the pharmacy, my first time walking around the quaint village. At the pharmacy, I got in line, prepared to wait my turn. And then, in the sea of white faces behind the counter, I noticed one Black woman. Our eyes connected. "I can take you at this register," she said, beckoning me to walk forward. Before the transaction was complete, she complimented me on my eyeglasses.

The line at the pharmacy was short; just one other person was ahead of me. And while I can't be certain, I imagine she thought "I don't see people like me in here that often, so I am going to take this opportunity to go out of my way for her." To be fair, I have had other experiences where people who do not look like me have done very similar things. But I sensed that Black woman, in that white town, was inspired by an inner knowing. In that glance, we both recognized the Black women who raised us, and because we love and value them, we had the capacity to love and value a complete stranger. She saw me; I wasn't overlooked or ignored. The Black woman's inner knowing prompted action and reinforced sisterhood.

* * *

For this book project, I partnered with the highly regarded Marist Poll for an exclusive national survey that included a representative sample of Black women. In October 2021, the poll was conducted in two stages—a phone survey representative of the US national adult population and an online probability panel survey of Black Americans. Both phone and online datasets were combined for a total of 2,161 Americans and balanced to ensure that each group was represented in proportion to the national population. An oversample of Black Americans (966) and Black women (619) was done to provide analysis of the groups' opinions.

The survey results support the idea that Black women hold other Black women and themselves in high regard. The data also shows the existence of a deep bond. Nearly eight in ten Black women agree that Black women are part of a sisterhood. Most Black women (83 percent) trust other Black women and nearly four in ten trust other Black women a great deal.

It is not an accident that eight in ten Black women trust other Black women. Rooted in Black women teaching younger generations to value and love themselves, trust is a natural outgrowth of the inner knowing. I trust Black women to esteem Black women. I trust Black women to defend the freedoms of Black women. I trust Black women to know, without question, that the lives of Black women matter. My trust also acknowledges that interactions between Black women are not universally harmonious; they can be harmful and hurtful. But based on my personal experiences, these negative intragroup relations are nullified by an inner knowing—when all hell breaks loose, Black women can trust other Black women to show up, have their back, and go to war.

The Marist Poll data also substantiates the optimism and confidence Black women possess. Most Black women (80 percent) agree with the statement that they see themselves as someone who has high self-esteem. And of that group, more than three in ten strongly agree with that statement. Along the same lines, most Black women (70 percent) say they have been successful in life. Most Black women (75 percent) believe they have it within their own power to succeed, and most (74 percent) agree that achieving success and recognition in their job or career is realistic. These results are notable because they break the stereotypes of lack that are still present in everyday discourse.

The Marist Poll results also demonstrate the tremendous value Black women have for themselves and other Black women. This is significant. It speaks to the success of Black mothers (and all Black women who serve in a mother capacity) who have taught their daughters to value themselves and to resist systems that degrade, demean, and dehumanize African-descendant women and girls. It is a testament to the spirt, heart, and agency of Black women to counteract and reject prevailing, pejorative narratives that misconstrue who Black women are and what they can do.

Throughout this book, I will posit that much of what the United States thinks about Black women is wrong. I will share surprising results from the data analyzed for this book. My primary sources, beyond interviews and archival literature, are the aforementioned Marist Poll results and the analysis of eighty[2] years of US census data gathered by the IPUMS USA project at the University of Minnesota. Globally renowned, IPUMS collects, preserves, and harmonizes US census and survey microdata from 1790 through the present. I met with the director of spatial analysis at IPUMS, David Van Riper, and asked for the university's help with collecting and tabulating US census data to understand Black women's success in the United States.

Both data sets explicitly transform negative normative conceptions of Black women by recognizing achievement and acknowledging their power to create meaningful lives.

* * *

The late Black feminist author and cultural critic bell hooks identified "imperialist white supremacist capitalist patriarchy"[3] as systems of oppression. "We can't begin to understand the nature of domination if we don't understand how these systems connect with one another . . . a global context . . . context of class, of empire, of capitalism, of racism and of patriarchy. Those things are all linked—an interlocking system."[4] hook's notion of an interlocking system of oppression is a foundational principle of this book. It not only explains the global social order, but the lived experiences of Black women in the United States.

At a Rutgers University sociologist conference in 2009, veteran scholar Dr. Elizabeth Higginbotham led a panel exploring the subject "Black women, sociologists, and work." In the introduction to the panel's conversation, Higginbotham acknowledged a particular labor of love:

> . . . like many Black women academics I was very excited about telling stories, especially putting down on paper, the work involved in creating scholarship that seeks to unravel many of the myths put into place to support our oppression. It is rewarding to labor to reveal the resiliency, the courage, and the thinking of Black women that has been obscured by these myths.[5]

The work to dispel myths about Black women is part of their legacy, one that this book aims to honor and push forward. It is a labor of love Black women have done for centuries. It is most evident by the late nineteenth century when larger numbers of Black women began to publish books and articles in newspapers, journals, and magazines.

In 1894, educator and journalist Gertrude Bustill Mossell published her first book, *The Work of the Afro-American Woman*. In this collection of essays and poems, Mossell "chronicled the achievements of thousands of black women in all different fields ... [the] list included information about black women's achievements in education, literature, journalism, medicine, law, missionary work, art, business, and music."[6]

The following year, Katherine D. Tillman published an essay in the *AME Church Review*, one of the earliest known Black journals. Tillman's essay, which established the contributions of Black women in "the great drama of Negro progress,"[7] was particularly relevant to postbellum colloquy. Tillman's essay included detailed examples of highly skilled and accomplished Black women—from artists, seamstresses, and entrepreneurs to historians, journalists, and medical doctors.

At one point, referencing the generosity of African descendant women, Tillman wrote that the first five dollars given to the Lincoln Memorial in Washington, DC, was donated by a formerly enslaved woman, Charlotte Cushman. Tillman, like me, was motivated to tell her truth about Black women, "We have been charged with mental inferiority; now if we can prove that with cultivated hearts and brains, we can accomplish the same that is accomplished by our fairer sisters of the Caucasian race, why then, we have refuted the falsehood."[8] Tillman desired to prove the intelligence of Black women—that they could be just as accomplished as white women.

In 1902, Susie King Taylor published the only account of a Black woman's wartime experience during the Civil War. In her memoir *Reminiscences of My Life in Camp*, Taylor recounted her service to the Union Army as a laundress, teacher, and a nurse for the 33rd US Colored Troops Infantry Regiment. Born enslaved in Georgia in 1848, Taylor did not want the participation of African descendant women in the Civil War to be forgotten:

> There are many people who do not know what some of the colored women did during the war. There were hundreds of them who assisted the Union soldiers by hiding them and helping them to escape. Many were punished for taking food to the prison stockades for the prisoners . . . Others assisted in various ways the Union army. These things should be kept in history before the people.[9]

A straight line can be drawn from Tillman, Mossell, and Taylor to Higginbotham and others like Paula Giddings—author of the seminal 1980s book *When and Where I Enter: The Impact of Black Women on Race and Sex in America*—to the 2020 publication of *A Black Women's History of the United States* by Daina Ramey Berry and Kali Nicole Gross. These works were authored in three different centuries, but each sought to chronicle the successes of Black women. They were motivated to myth-bust, to share stories that would encourage Black women, and to inform a wider audience about their accomplishments.

Myth-busting is a difficult, seemingly never-ending endeavor. Higginbotham asserted that as soon as myths about Black women are dispelled, "new ones emerge."[10] However, I argue that many of the old myths have yet to be vanquished—the passage of time serves only to multiply the myth-buster's work. And so, I am compelled to join my foremothers and contemporaries in doing the work to eradicate false conceptions of Black women and to share stories of triumph.

There are different ways to dispel these myths. In 1895 Tillman found it "necessary to point out the leading ladies and the 'hits' that they have made."[11] She accomplished this task by naming specific Black women, their successes, and, in some cases, their city or state of residence. Her reporting was detailed, "Ida Gray, of Cincinnati . . . the only dentist that we have as yet, but there is a young AfroAmerican woman in Des Moines, a Miss Lizzie Weaver, who is engaged in the study of dentistry."[12] The painstakingly detailed, fact-based account speaks to Tillman's understanding that without her efforts and that of other Black women to chronicle their accomplishments, it would be lost to history.

Traditionally, Black women sociologists have dispelled myths by engaging and challenging the academy to research, study, and formulate theories that center Black women. But too often data has been employed to substantiate myths. Therefore, my chosen method of myth-busting is grounded in data—its collection, tabulation, and analysis.

* * *

At the start of writing this book, I asked a fundamental question: Why are white men and women the standard for comparison when evaluating Black women? While I support the idea of parity and the importance of knowing how groups compare to the "majority," this method does not provide the full scope of what it means to be a Black woman in the United States. To get the answer to my question, I first collaborated with the aforementioned University of Minnesota's IPUMS USA project to gather and tabulate US census data.

My approach was based on three core objectives: first, employ a methodology to evaluate Black women that adheres to scientific processes, but differs from the academy. To do this, we compared Black women against Black women over an extended period of time. My second objective was to determine variables. I focused on a nearly eighty-year[13] span (1940–2019) to capture data points pertaining to success. To determine success, I used variables employed by sociologists: median annual wages, educational attainment, and occupation. I am not suggesting that one's wages, educational attainment, and occupation are the only, or even the best, determinants of success, but it is essential for me to explore areas society generally agrees are markers of "making it." For the third objective, although I do not advocate comparing Black women to other groups, it was important to understand how groups performed in relation to one another. Given the census's limited categorization of race in 1940, I chose to look at a total of four groups: Black women and men and white women and men.

Additionally, to ensure parity on educational levels, occupations, and median annual wages across the eighty-year timespan of analysis, all variables were tabulated for people ages twenty-five to sixty-four.

Once I had the data in hand, I enlisted the help of Dr. Constance F. Citro, senior scholar for the Committee on National Statistics at the National Academies of Sciences, Engineering, and Medicine, to help me analyze the data provided by the University of Minnesota. An octogenarian, Dr. Citro's long and storied career has been devoted to improving federal statistics for the public good.

DATA TREND ANALYSIS

Since 1940—despite fluctuations in labor market institutions, wages, and macroeconomic trends, changes in the supply and demand for workers, and shifts in workplace organization and practices—Black women ages twenty-five to sixty-four grew their median annual wage ten times (or 1000 percent) from 1940 to 2019. In contrast, as indicated in Graph A on the next page, accounting for the same variables, the annual median wages for Black men grew 600 percent and for white women and men just over 300 percent. While Black women have earned less than Black men and white women and men since 1940, the growth rate is remarkable. All of the figures I cite have been adjusted for inflation.

GRAPH A

Similarly, Black women have experienced high rates of growth in completing at least one year of college and at least four years of college. In 1940, just 4 percent of Black women ages twenty-five to sixty-four had completed at least one year of college. By 2019, as Graph B illustrates, the number of Black women completing at least one year of college grew fifteen times (1500 percent). Black women exceeded the growth rate of Black men (1400 percent), white women (600 percent), and white men (500 percent).

Congruently, 27 percent of Black women ages twenty-five to sixty-four completed four years or more of college in 2019, as did 34 percent of white men and 39 percent of white women. But Graph C shows that even though a higher percentage of white men and women completed four years or more of college, Black women had the highest rate of growth (1900 percent) over the eighty-year span of the four groups analyzed.

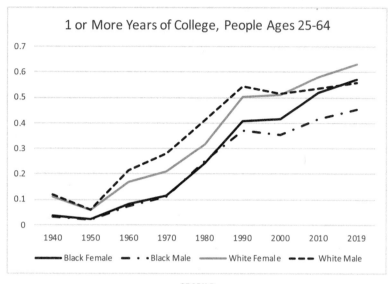

GRAPH B

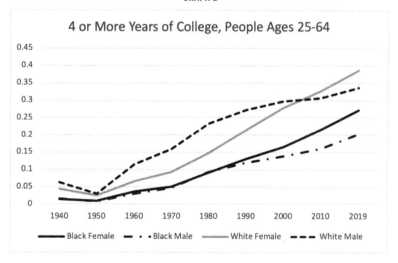

GRAPH C

The data I analyzed grouped adults ages twenty-five to sixty-four who reported their occupation (those with a job currently or with a recent job) into five occupational groups. The only occupation not included is farming, which never occupied more than 10 percent of any of the four groups analyzed except for Black men in 1940 and 1950. For Black women, I focused on three occupational sectors most important for that group.

In 1940, almost 70 percent of Black women ages twenty-five to sixty-four who worked in the past year were service workers (most in private households). As demonstrated in Graph D, just a quarter of Black women (26 percent) were service workers in 2019.

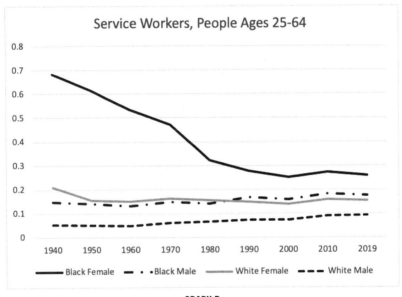

GRAPH D

Across the eighty-year time span of the analysis, Graph E shows clerical and sales workers have been the province of women. Thirty percent of white women were in this category in 1940 and almost as many are still in this category today. For Black women, the percentage in this category rose dramatically—there were fourteen times (1400 percent) as many Black women clerical and sales workers in 2019 as in 1940, likely reflecting movement from service jobs.

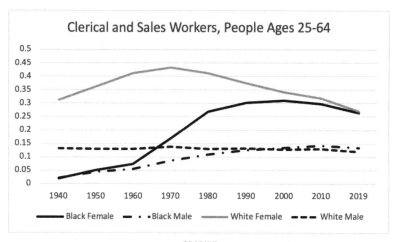

GRAPH E

The professional, technical, and manager jobs, as represented in Graph F, saw significant growth in all four groups. Both Black and white women showed the highest growth rates, seven and eight times respectively as many workers in the sector in 2019 as in 1940. In 2019, 51 percent of white women and 42 percent of white men were in professional roles as were 38 percent of Black women. But the number of Black women in professional roles grew faster (700 percent) than it did for white men (300 percent) over the eighty-year span.

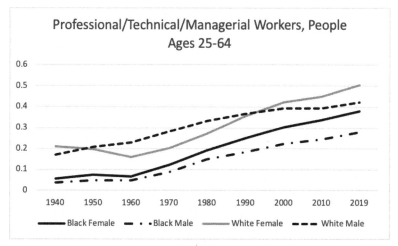

GRAPH F

Some may struggle with the optimistic prism through which the census data has been interpreted. I realize that from 1940 to 2019 Black women have earned less than all the groups examined here. And it is true that in 2019 more white women completed four or more years of college than Black women and more white men and women hold professional, technical, and manager roles than do Black women. My objective is not to ignore reality. But I know a white supremacist, patriarchal worldview frames data in a way that supports the superiority of white men. I seek to reframe how we talk about the successes of Black women alongside the oppressive realities that challenge Black women and other marginalized groups in the United States. I frankly have no interest in maintaining the status quo.

The data results present a collective win for every single person who has identified as a Black woman on the US census since 1940. This feat could not have been done alone—Black women did it together. And while it is true that Black women's rate of growth over the last eighty years is impressive, most Black women have earned their achievements while blindfolded, with their hands tied behind their backs and their legs cut off at the knees.

* * *

In one fluid motion, a distraught young woman sat down on an outdoor bench, carelessly discarding a tan Spelman tote bag. It was a sweltering spring day in Atlanta, March 2004.

Alisha Gordon sat alone, sobbing inconsolably. Tears rolled down cheeks colored by melanin. Moments earlier, at the college infirmary, Gordon learned the results of a blood test: she was pregnant.

In the throes of disbelief, Gordon glanced at the tossed tote. An application to a graduate journalism program was visible at the top of the bag. As Gordon realized her future had been irrevocably altered, words, unbound by anguish, tumbled out: "That's never going to happen!"[14] But there was no one to hear her exclamation, witness the death of her dream, or mourn it's untimely passing.

A few months later, Gordon graduated from Spelman College two months pregnant. She moved back to Decatur, the Georgia city of her birth and childhood. A dark, Cimmerian period followed.

Fearful of the unknown and hesitant to raise a child on her own, Gordon asked the baby's father to relocate from Memphis. It was a devastating mistake. After the move, he became violent: physical and verbal abuses were a regular occurrence. Once, when Gordon was six months pregnant, he wielded a kitchen knife and yelled, "Well if you gon' leave me, you gon' leave a dead woman!"[15] before he chased her out of the apartment. Deeply ashamed, at the time Gordon hid the abuse from everyone:

> The night before [our baby shower] we get into an argument, and he tries to choke me. He misses and scratches up the side of my face. Three big scratches on the side of my face. But I had to go to the baby shower and people were like "what happened to your face?" [and] I just smiled for the cameras.[16]

Shortly after their daughter was born, Gordon walked away from the relationship. A newly single mom, she worked various odd jobs and eventually landed a role as a high school English teacher in Douglas County. She loved the work, but it was difficult to raise her daughter on $34,000 a year: " . . . daycare was $600 a month and my rent was $625 a month, so I still qualified for food stamps. And there were a couple of times when our lights got cut off and I was getting eviction notices."[17]

Despite a full-time job and the support of public assistance, Gordon and her daughter were chronically housing and food insecure. These traumas formed and crystalized Gordon's framing, normalizing a perception that she did not simply *receive* welfare, but *embodied* welfare. And for more than a decade, Gordon's self-deprecatory description "welfare single mom"[18] was a regular refrain.

Harshly stigmatized in the United States, the trope is exacerbated by the confluence of race, class, gender, and the demonization of underserved groups. In the 1980s, "welfare queen" became synonymous with Black women—lazy, promiscuous, unwed mothers swindling hard-working taxpayers. Although white people and the working poor are the largest recipients of welfare,[19] "welfare queen" remains a stubbornly entrenched Black woman stereotype, like the equally damaging antecedents: Mammy, Jezebel, Sapphire, and Beulah.

In December 2010, Gordon felt she was not fulfilling her life's purpose and she began to pray, "Lord, is there something else I should be doing?"[20] When the school district announced teacher furloughs the following spring, Gordon saw it as her moment to do something. Months later, she resigned—to the chagrin of her family. And at twenty-nine, she and her daughter moved in with her mother.

A few months later, on September 21, 2011, Gordon wrote an open letter to the state of Georgia, petitioning the governor to stay the execution of Troy Davis, a Black man on death row for the 1989 killing of a police officer, a crime he maintained he never committed. Gordon posted the blog online. It went viral and "became the first time that I would enter into public discourse about social justice and the death penalty."[21] Although Davis was executed, the experience motivated Gordon to start blogging regularly about the intersection of social justice and faith. Inspired by her writings, a friend urged Gordon to apply to the Candler School of Theology at Emory University. The leap of faith paid off when she was accepted into the program. "I was hype! I started going to school full time and that decision changed the entire trajectory of my life."[22]

Gordon graduated from Emory in 2015, and a year after graduation, she accepted a job offer from a prominent, faith-based women's organization as the new executive director of spiritual growth. It was a dream job, located in a metropolis known for dream-making, and it paid substantially more. The New York City move heralded another notable new: for the first time in her young life, Gordon's eleven-year-old daughter no longer needed public assistance. The shift in circumstances engendered a seismic shift in Gordon's perspective:

> I remember saying to somebody, you know I am a welfare single mom. And I caught myself and said, "Bitch, no you're not! No, you're not!" But I had to do this . . . reimaging of the narrative to say, "I utilized public assistance to shape and recreate and reimagine what my life could be." That's a very different perspective than saying, "woe is me I'm going to get this government check." What does it mean to say that as a Black single mother I am the most innovative motherfucker I know?[23]

In Gordon's story, I noticed the tenor and tone, the contour and shape, the semantics of words. I heard the ancestral reverb in the depths beneath voice. And I recognized the inner knowing in Gordon's narrative.

* * *

Scholars believe lived experiences, choices, and interactions with others frame an individual's perception of the world. Reframing is the process of shifting one's perception about something or someone, usually in a more positive, optimistic direction.

Reframing is a technique regularly used by psychotherapists to help patients look at relationships, circumstances, or themselves in a new way. Marketers and advertisers employ reframing to sway public sentiment about a company or product.

For innovation experts like Thomas Wedell-Wedellsborg, reframing solves problems: "the point of reframing is not to find the 'real' problem but, rather, to see if there is a better one to solve."[24] To reframe a problem depends, he says, on an "ability to question our own beliefs and to challenge assumptions that we may have held onto for a long time."[25] It is not easy to recognize, question, and then reframe long-held, ingrained beliefs, but Black women, like Gordon, have shown that it is possible.

Gordon grew up in the 1980s and 1990s in Decatur, Georgia, in a two-parent, working-class home. Life centered around their conversative southern missionary Baptist church, where her dad served as a trustee and deacon. After church on Sundays, Gordon's family ate at the Piccadilly Restaurant at the South DeKalb Mall. In the summers, they vacationed in Panama City Beach, Florida. Intelligent and outgoing, Gordon played the piano, participated in gymnastics, and excelled in school. Although Gordon did not describe her childhood as "bad,"[26] it was not without strife. When she was twelve or thirteen years old, her idyllic childhood was upended by her parents' divorce:

> I would spend my eighth, ninth, and maybe tenth grade
> years skipping school, sleeping with all these types of

different boys, trying to grasp at these breadcrumbs of male attention, which happens for a lot of Black girls, when they have this tear in their paternal relationship. I went on a two-year stint where I drove my mom up a wall being a fake badass. And then I finally turned the corner in the eleventh grade, and I was just getting my shit together. Because I was always a high achieving student, I got accepted to Spelman early decision.[27]

Gordon's perceptions were framed by the pressures to succeed that come with being a first-generation college student. When choices incongruous with her strict southern Baptist upbringing led to single motherhood, and underemployment led to welfare, shame and regret were constant companions.

Gordon's framing was further constructed by intersectionality. First coined in 1989 by law professor Kimberlé Crenshaw, intersectionality provides a way to understand the Black woman's experience as an intersection, and thereby exacerbation, of inequalities. Overlapping, synchronous oppressions—race, class, sexuality, gender—deepen and harden negative frames. Reframing for Black women becomes an act of resistance. An act of power.

Reframing is how Gordon's self-talk shifted from "welfare single mom" to "most innovative motherfucker I know." And whether it is private (like Gordon's) or public, reframing is essential to creating lives that sustain and nourish Black women.

The famed Aesop fable *The Hare and the Tortoise* is a metaphor for reframing. The familiar childhood story can be summarized in a few sentences. The Hare thought it ridiculous that the Tortoise wanted to race him, the fastest animal in the forest, but he accepted the challenge. In the middle of the race, the over-confident Hare decided to take a nap. But the slow and steady Tortoise continued to plod along—eventually passing the slumbering Hare. When the Hare woke up, the Tortoise was so close to the finish line that the race was effectively over. Against conventional wisdom and expectation, the Tortoise beat the Hare.

In the context of the story, Black women are represented by the Tortoise and society, the Hare. Tortoises are hindered by the reality that they are one of the slowest creatures on Earth, moving at a rate of less than half a mile per hour. Black women are hindered by the realities of enslavement and systemic intersectional oppressions.

But like the Tortoise, Black women have kept moving, not because they are superhuman, never get tired, or can carry every burden. Black women keep moving forward because their dreams, ideas, and visions are greater than the forces trying to slow them down. Black women persist because they love their children, families, and communities. Black women persevere because they can.

* * *

The ability to reframe myths is grounded in concepts of identity and consciousness held by descendants of enslaved Africans. It is a phenomenon articulated by W.E.B. Du Bois in his early twentieth century book *The Souls of Black Folk*. Du Bois named the duality of the Black experience as a double consciousness:

> It is a peculiar sensation, this double consciousness, this sense of always looking at one's self [*sic*] through the eyes of others, of measuring one's soul by the tape of a world that looks on in amused contempt and pity. One ever feels

his [or her] twoness—an American, a Negro: two souls, two thoughts, two unreconciled strivings; two warring ideals in one dark body.[28]

Described by Du Bois as a "second-sight," double consciousness enables Black women to understand how they're viewed by society, in general, and by white people, specifically.

More than a century later, a dear friend from my college years expanded on Du Bois' work. In her second book, *Stories of Identity among Black, Middle Class, Second Generation Caribbeans*, Dr. Yndia S. Lorick-Wilmot introduced a new theoretical framework, Triple Identity Consciousness. Lorick-Wilmot posited that Triple Identity Consciousness provided a more accurate understanding of how Black women negotiate identity in a world that does not value their humanity or contributions:

> DuBois' framework suggests there is a duality of consciousness the African descendant possess in order to circumvent the effects and consequences of racial discrimination and subjugation, that is rather limiting. Instead, developing Triple Identity Consciousness, I argue that African descendants are acutely aware of this identity duality, yet engage in a third level of consciousness. This third level of consciousness is the intentional act of subverting this haunting experience into one that is about radical identity. But there is a process by which African descendants must contend with and the ways Black people perpetuate these identifications while devising ways to subvert or claim Blackness in more positively meaningful ways. Triple Identity Consciousness is the "thing" that goads action. Action to enhance your life and the lives of others.[29]

Reframing myths about Black women is Triple Identity Consciousness in action—it is the "intentional act of subverting" myths. It is Black women creating narratives and perceptions of themselves, in the likeness of their inner knowing.

The national Marist Poll study reveals a dichotomy between Black women's perception of their value and potential and how Black women understand society's perception of their value and contributions. As noted earlier, most Black women say they have been successful in life and 74 percent report that achieving success and recognition in their job or career is realistic. However, nearly 90 percent of Black women say that their successes are generally overlooked and ignored by society and nearly eight in ten (78 percent) feel that Black women have less opportunity in life than other groups in society have.

The tension in the survey results, Black women feeling successful v. their success being ignored by society, is reflective of the Triple Identity Consciousness theory. Black women are aware of how they view themselves (capable of success) and how society treats them (overlooked, incapable of success). And Triple Identity Consciousness says, not only do I see how you see me, but I am going to exercise my agency to create a life that is meaningful to me. And in so doing, Black women have been able to rise—proof of inherent power.

* * *

Like the Tortoise, Alisha Gordon placed one foot in the front of the other, empowered by her love as a mother and a dream that she was meant for more.

Today, Gordon's daughter is seventeen, and like her mom she is headed to Spelman College, one of the top historically Black colleges and universities (HBCUs) in the country. As for

Gordon, she is an ordained reverend, activist, political organizer, and the founder and executive director of the Current
Project. Born out of her lived experiences, the organization supports Black single mothers by helping them attain and maintain
economic stability:

> The approach we take is an innovative one because we
> don't do crisis work, we're not giving out diapers or all that
> kind of stuff. We address the "middler moms," women
> who are one decision away from being on the other side of
> surviving or thriving.[30]

Gordon defines the "middler mom" as someone who is one
step away from a breakthrough. Ultimately her organization is
focused on being a bridge for Black single mothers so they can do
what she's done: thrive. Despite the hopelessness she felt nearly
twenty years ago, Gordon's dreams did not die. They expanded
and grew. Gordon's reframing from "welfare mom" to "the most
innovative motherfucker" is a blueprint for other Black women
to follow.

* * *

This book is written for any person who identifies as a Black
femme—regardless of sexual preference and/or gender designa-
tion. I hope to be in conversation with all Black women, but my
views do not represent all Black women. First, Black women are
a polylith. And second, my *weltanschauung* is formed by my personal experiences and choices.

   I affirm the right of Black women to choose. Be it fascist or
Marxist, conservative or liberal, carnivore or herbivore, extro-
vert or ambivert, rapper or rocker. I believe Black women can

wear their hair natural, in knotless braids, or a weave. I fundamentally believe Black women should live their lives in ways that bring joy.

I do not tackle sexual/intimate relationships in this book—heterosexual, pansexual, same sex, or otherwise. As a Black, heterosexual woman, I am personally interested in romantic relationships, but the topic has been written and discussed ad nauseam in Black culture and I do not have anything to add to the discourse at this time. Instead, I contend with patriarchy and the power dynamics between Black men and women.

The major themes explored in this book are the notions of success, power, and the collective strength of Black women. In the United States, success is largely defined by external factors. As previously noted, sociologists determine the socio-economic status of an individual or group of people based on educational attainment, income, and type of employment.

While I measure Black women against this academic standard, I also define success as the ability of Black women to create a life that brings satisfaction. No two people share the exact same dreams, goals, or motivations. I know Black women who have redefined, broadened, and stretched what it means to be successful. I also know many Black women who are highly accomplished and successful in ways we tend to define success. Regardless of whether success is exemplified in raising children, fighting for social justice, graduating from college, or as Mary J. Blige put it in an interview on the ABC News program *The View*, attaining "peace of mind;"[31] I will show that Black women believe they can (and they often do) achieve their definition of success.

German sociologist Max Weber defined power as an "ability to control others, events, or resources; to make happen what one wants to happen in spite of obstacles, resistance, or opposition."[32] The question this book will explore is how Black women can use their power to bring about the greatest good. I view power as Black women reaching higher and holding positions of authority and influence in public and private spheres. My position makes some Black women uncomfortable due to the devastating impact of intersecting, dominating power structures. I believe that knowing what one wants and going after it doesn't have to be at the expense of others when there's a motivation of love, collaboration, and goodwill toward humanity.

One of my younger cousins recently graduated from Stanford Law School, passed the California Bar Exam on the first try, and is currently working at a prestigious law firm. Kind and thoughtful, she had a challenging goal, she achieved it, and I am extremely proud of her.

I asked my cousin to read portions of this book in various stages of the writing process. On the topic of power and success, she shared, "It made me nervous thinking about all of the pressure to succeed; why can't I just live in a nice house with a white picket fence and live quietly?" I empathize with her sentiment. She's worked extremely hard against great odds to achieve, but despite her success, she feels conflicted about how high she should reach, how far she should go. Why, she wonders, should there be more required of her? I gave great thought to her question because I know her concerns are shared by many Black women. My advice was straightforward, "don't strive beyond what is in your heart to achieve."

Research has shown that the social and cultural pressure for Black women to be strong has had a negative psychological and physiological impact. In a study exploring Black women's views on stress, strength, and health, a participant echoed my cousin's sentiments, "People always say, oh you look so calm . . . and I'm thinking I'm just about to crumble in two seconds and I think a lot of people don't know when Black women are stressed because of the superwoman syndrome . . . "[33]

A recent article in *Essence* magazine reported on the increased stress Black women felt during the coronavirus pandemic:

> Women, especially Black women, deal with something called superwoman phenomenon where you're already dealing with and caring for so many other people and that's been worsened by the pandemic. They're putting themselves and their wellness second to everyone else's . . . This is important to highlight because it's not only emotional stress you're feeling but it can actually physically affect your heart strength and sometimes lead to death.[34]

I've considered these factors in my urgent call to Black women to acknowledge and wield their power. I define the wielding of power as not only about becoming the CEO or being the "perfect" mother; it is also about knowing when to say no, knowing when to rest, and knowing when to put your health and well-being ahead of the expectations of families, jobs, and culture. Black women have had to be strong, and that strength has helped them, but it has also caused pain. Resilience and perseverance without self-care is deadly.

* * *

This book is conceptually divided into three parts. The first section uses new analysis of eighty years of census data, findings from the exclusive Marist Poll, and personal narratives to prove that Black women are not only successful but flourishing.

The second section critically examines the effectiveness of our historical allies—Black men and white women—in the fight for freedom. I urge Black women to look outside of the United States to forge transnational alliances with Afro-descendant Black women throughout the Americas. The third section recognizes, affirms, and dissects Black women's power.

Each chapter revolves around a central argument: Black women are rising. If Black women own that, they will run the world.

In this chapter (chapter one), I tell the truth about Black women, who we are and what we've accomplished. Relying on the new analysis of US census data and the Marist Poll results, I show that Black women's rate of success in higher education, income, and occupational status far exceeds assumed expectations.

The second chapter explains the *secret sauce*. It is my explanation for how Black women have done so well, despite systemic, intersectional oppressions. The *secret sauce* doesn't erase pain or eliminate the cost of resilience, but it acts as a shock absorber, providing the inner strength to rise.

In the third chapter, I introduce a new theory called the Lemonade Lifestyle. It is analogous to a formula, a methodology for living with intention, and is marked by courage, agency, and audacity.

In the fourth chapter, I confront Black patriarchy and the ways in which (too many) Black women push Black men forward by stepping backward. Ceding power that was and is rightfully theirs. From the Black Church to the nuclear family and social movements, Black women have been leading from behind. Their babies, their men, their boys taking precedence, overshadowing what Black women want, what they need, and the full, unfettered exercise of their gifts and talents.

The fifth chapter deals with the complicated relationship between Black women and white women. I will explain why many Black women distrust white women. I also examine if it benefits Black women to seek allyship with white women or whether it is time for Black women to accept what is and move on to more fruitful and mutually beneficial alliances.

In the sixth chapter, I argue that Black women can achieve full parity if they partner with other African descendant women who carry the legacy of the trans-Atlantic slave trade, enslavement, and the continued trauma of racial *and* gender discrimination. By cultivating and sustaining partnerships that unite all Afro-descendant women—those living in the Americas and elsewhere—a new, powerful, global coalition will emerge.

The seventh chapter explores Black women and power. I present real-world examples that demonstrate our power. And I explain how Black women's power diverges from notions of power defined by Western, white male philosophers.

The eighth chapter brings the data, frameworks, and narratives together in a way that celebrates Black women.

As a daughter of the Deep South, great-granddaughter of Georgia sharecroppers, and a succedent of enslaved Africans, I carry the enslavement of my foremothers. At times it manifests physically. A groaning in my soul, nightmares in my dreams. Unfortunately, I am not alone. From the Holocaust to enslavement, "an emerging line of research is exploring how historical and cultural traumas"[35] are akin to worthless heirlooms passed down through the generations.

Like millions of Black women, I have not been spared what it means and is to be a Black woman in the United States—and yet, I, WE, RISE.

CHAPTER 2

SECRET SAUCE

The YouTube video momentarily flickered. Soon, an image of a stately, majestic woman stood expectantly in the center of the pulpit. As the music cued to begin, her rich, full contralto enveloped the packed church, filling the congregants with the sound of her signature voice.

That night, the legendary "Queen of Gospel," Mahalia Jackson, performed a soulful rendition of the popular hymn "How I Got Over." As the Black communicants nodded their heads and swayed in rhythm to the music, Jackson masterfully ad-libbed: "How I got over? /How did I make it over?/You know my soul look back and wonder/How did I make it over?"[1]

The hymn's title, "How I Got Over," is contemporaneously a question and a declaration of victory. It asks: How does one possibly get through difficult circumstances? And the answer implies—because it is written in the past tense—that one will *make it over.*

Undisclosed is the obstacle that needs overcoming, the trouble that needs remedying. But for Black folks, Black women in particular, an explanation is not needed. They are acutely aware of what it means to be Black women in the United States.

Black women have scars. Etched on souls, coded in DNA, seared in memory. Four hundred years enslaved. Four hundred years dehumanized. And they understand how history foments present-day, reoccurring traumas.

The expectation of victory—implicit in the song's opening lyrics—signals to an audience to prepare for a clap-your-hands, stomp-your-feet testimony at the hymn's culmination. A tradition rooted in Baptist, Pentecostal, and other denominations of the Black Christian Church, "testifying" is the public act of sharing the good things God has done for you and your loved ones. While no longer ubiquitous, it typically occurs at a predetermined time during a church service. Anyone in attendance can take the opportunity to stand up before the congregation to give a praise report, read a Bible verse, or sing a song.

Testimonies can lead to exuberant demonstrations of worship that Black churchgoers call "getting happy." And "getting happy" is accompanied by fast-paced feet-stomping music while folks shout and dance up and down the aisles.

Jackson's gritty, explosive sound "was rooted in Baptist Pentecostal music"[2] and in the "blues and jazz stylings"[3] she was exposed to during her upbringing in New Orleans. A passionate performer, Jackson would often sing so hard and with such deep conviction that her hair style was unrecognizable by the end of a concert.

That night as she sang, it became clear Jackson was doing more than singing, she was giving her testimony.

You know, I come to thank God this evening
I come to thank Him, this evening
You know all, all night long
God kept His angels watching over me

And early this morning, early this morning
God told His angels
God said, "Touch her in my name"
God said, "Touch her in my name"[4]

As Jackson "got happy," she clapped her hands and walked from one end of the pulpit to the other. And by the end of the song, she had completely abandoned the lyrics. Common in gospel music, repetition does three things: emphasize the miraculous, ensure listeners haven't missed an important revelation, and demonstrates the singer's skills.

I rose this morning
I rose this morning
I rose this morning
I feel like shouting
I feel like shouting
I feel like shouting
I feel like shouting
I feel like shouting
I feel like shouting
I feel like shouting[5]

By this point, some congregants in the video were standing, swaying back and forth, raising their hands in worship. But Jackson was no longer singing for her fellow brothers and sisters in Christ, but directly to and for God.

I just got to thank God
I just got to thank God
I just got to thank God
I just got to thank Him

Thank God for being so, God been good to me, yeah[6]

At the end of the hymn, Jackson slowed the tempo down. Expertly elongating every syllable of every word; in total command of the congregants and her voice.

"How I Got Over" was written and first performed by Jackson's friend Clara Ward, lead of the gospel ensemble Clara Ward Singers. The Ward Singers, which initially included Ward's mother Gertrude Murphy Ward and sister Willa Ward-Royster, was a popular gospel group in the 1940s–1960s. In her autobiography, Ward-Royster shared the seminal event that led Ward to write "How I Got Over."

In 1951, the Clara Ward Singers were driving through Georgia enroute to a singing engagement in Atlanta when they stopped at a service station to stretch their legs and fill up the gas tank. Ward-Royster wrote that the white gas attendant seemed offended by their car and began calling them "niggers . . . [then] three other men popped out of the doorway and started excitedly exclaiming to each other about [the] Cadillac—how large, roomy, and pretty it was."[7] The men accused the group of women of stealing the car and called Ward's mother a "thieving black bitch."[8]

Before the situation worsened, the group of women hopped in their car and sped away without purchasing gas. About half a mile down the road, an open-backed truck filled with several white men sitting in the back blocked them from driving farther. As they anxiously stopped, the men circled the Cadillac, forcing the women to get out of the car; "Black shitty niggers,"[9] they taunted, "let us see you buck dance. If we think you dance good enough, we might allow you all to crawl away from here. Dance niggers, dance!"[10]

Ward's mother—in a flash of inspiration—pretended to be possessed by a demon, "Her face was contorted, eyes bulging and tongue flicking like a serpent's. She let out a shriek and yelled, 'Oh Prince of Darkness, come to the aid of your faith servant . . . smite those and their children who defy and berate Thee and me.'"[11] The ruse worked. The men ran off, afraid of being cursed. The Ward Singers escaped, physically unscathed.

But the racist encounter impacted Clara Ward emotionally. Soon after, as described by her sister Ward-Royster, she began to talk about the "hardship, injustice, brutality, and the inhumanity of slavery. 'My Lord, those poor slaves,' she would say, moved to gentle, sympathetic tears, 'they had to have been extremely strong emotionally and unshakable in their faith to face and survive each new, horrible day.'"[12] Later that year, the experience in Georgia propelled Ward to rewrite and record "How I Got Over."

A prolific composer, Ward wrote hundreds of gospel songs before she died of a stroke in 1973. "How I Got Over" was one of her most successful. Not only has the hymn been sung by gospel great Yolanda Adams and recorded by the "Queen of Soul" Aretha Franklin, but Mahalia Jackson also performed the song at the 1963 March on Washington for Jobs and Freedom before 250,000 people. "How I Got Over" is more than a song; it is a testimony reminding Black women that they can overcome hardships they uniquely face.

In chapter one, I reframed the pejorative stereotypes of Black women by reporting on their untold story of triumph and ascendance. The data I presented documents that Black women have not been stymied, but have advanced, despite intersectional oppressions.

Consider the following. When the racist group of white men surrounded and taunted the Ward Singers, Clara Ward was so afraid she crouched on the floor of the car and hid under a blanket so they would not see her. Yet Ward is also the same woman who channeled that terrifying and degrading experience into writing a song of victory. How did Clara Ward take a gendered, racist attack in Deep South Georgia and turn it into power? Black women, like Ward, have learned to turn fear, hardship, and oppression into victory. How we do that is worthy of exploration.

The ways in which Black women "get over" is due to what I call our *secret sauce*—the source of our resilience, endurance, and fortitude. The sauce explains how Black women have achieved success and live fulfilling lives *despite* the noose of oppression. The *secret sauce* doesn't erase the pain of racism, sexism, or classism, nor does it ease the cost of resilience. Rather, it acts as a shock absorber, emboldening Black woman to face another day and to continue the fight for full freedom.

The *secret sauce* is a strategy born in slavery—a legacy passed from generation to generation: mother to daughter, aunt to niece, grandmother to granddaughter. As a survival mechanism, it enables Black women to do much with little, in ways big and small. The Black women's *secret sauce* is comprised of four key components: our foremothers, creativity, faith, and sisterhood.

While I was raised to keep family business in the family, it is necessary to share the secret of our resilience, so it's never forgotten. Black girls need to know that Black women thrive. Black girls need to embrace the idea that Black women and girls should never be underestimated. And most importantly, Black girls need to understand their innate capacity to rise.

It is our foremothers who illustrate, in thought, word, and deed, how Black women "get over."

FOREMOTHERS

My paternal grandmother is looking forward to her one hundredth birthday. She still has a few years to go, but at ninety-three, she expects to make it. For my part, I've promised to throw a bigger bash than the ninetieth fête held in her honor.

The granddaughter of slaves and the daughter of a sharecropper, Anna Jewel Barnette's story is a love song—a testament that life is a journey of learning to love oneself. Only when self-love is mastered can we come to terms with our fallibility, wholeheartedly love others, and live a life of purpose. Standing five feet tall (in heels), Grannymama, as my sisters and I call her, has the sweetest southern drawl you've ever heard. It's like warm, homemade banana bread paired with a steaming cup of coffee. "Hey, how you doin?" She asks every time I call. She has a head full of white, fluffy hair, twinkling eyes, and beautiful, wrinkle-free dark skin.

On May 21, 1929, Grannymama was born at home in Oconee County, Georgia, to Sidney and Lola Thurmond. Her father's pet name for her was Black Gal, an endearment my grandmother remembers fondly. When she was a little girl, her family moved to Athens, approximately seventy miles northeast of Atlanta.

As an adult, my grandmother decided to stay in Athens, a city where she raised my father and uncle, worked for thirty years as an insurance agent, and for more than sixty years continues to be an active member of Hill First Baptist Church. Our family often teases that she is the true mayor of Athens—she knows everyone, and everyone knows and honors her.

My grandmother's proximity to a century on this Earth belies a robust lifestyle of service. Today she participates in the following organizations: Northwestern Baptist Association No. 1, Church Women United, Veterans of Foreign Wars Post 3910, Athens-Clarke County Democratic Committee, and the 1967 Class Mother of the Burney-Harris High School (where my dad and uncle earned their diplomas).

For me and countless others she is a true wonder. Smart as a whip, with a great sense of humor, Grannymama is sassy, outspoken, and delightfully mischievous. Full of health and vitality, she still lives on her own and takes care of herself. It's very easy to admire my grandmother, but I know her story and the marvelous human she is today took decades to become.

My grandmother's first husband was an alcoholic, verbally and physically abusive, and a serial cheater. Back then, she didn't have a lot of confidence, "I had always given in to everything . . . and then go somewhere in a corner and cry."[13] After more than twenty years, she divorced him when he refused to help their sons go to college, "When my boys were born, I always wanted them to go to college. And nothing was going to stop me from them going. He didn't want them to go, and I realized 'you know what, I can't help them and fight him too. Somebody got to go!'"[14] That one act of defiance awakened and affirmed an inner, preexisting strength:

> And that helped me to be the person I am now. Because now you have to deal with me. I had never been outspoken. I guess I kept all those things bottled up. Now, you don't have to worry how I feel, because I tell you what I think and how I feel. I don't mean any harm being that way, but I don't have headaches because I keep things bottled up. If something needs to be said I just tell you and I go to bed at night and go to sleep. I move on from the situation. That's what women have to do.[15]

I love to visit Grannymama, especially when it's just the two of us. I get to soak up all the wisdom oozing out of every pore. After one such visit in 2017, I was particularly inspired. As I waited for my flight to JFK to board, I ordered a glass of wine, and I began writing down the "bits of wisdom" I'd gleaned from my visit:

- Live a clean life (avoid drugs, smoking, excessive drinking)
- Work hard and stay busy
- Have a positive outlook
- Help people and love them with your actions
- Be forgiving
- Surround yourself with people who can help you grow
- Be honest and people will be drawn to you
- Speak your mind
- Don't let people take advantage of you; stand up for yourself
- Don't play when it comes to money
- Stay adventurous
- Be independent
- Never give up
- Life is for the living

Grannymama's prescription for life is simple and exquisite, absent of bitterness and gall. Framed historically—from her gaze—it is profound. These ideas originate from a Black woman who has lived in the Deep South for nearly a century, worked the cotton fields with her sharecropping father, endured the indignities of the Jim Crow era, and was unable to vote until the Voting Rights Act passed in 1965, when she was in her mid-thirties.

My grandmother does not believe she is inferior to anyone. Although she does not have a "formal education," she asserts her right to be seen and heard. It is a manifestation of power to embody the ethos: "Life is for the living." That is radical. That is power. That is strength. And she is why I am strong.

The "Strong Black Woman" stereotype, the idea that Black women have superhuman mental, physical, and emotional strength, is complicated. The cultural trope is a double-edged sword, an inspiration and burden. A study published in the *Annals of the New York Academy of Sciences* in 2019 revealed:

> In the face of high levels of racial discrimination, some aspects of the superwoman persona, including feeling an obligation to present an image of strength and to suppress one's emotions, seemed to be protective of health, diminishing the negative health effects of chronic racial discrimination. But other facets of the persona, such as having an intense drive to succeed and feeling an obligation to help others, seemed to be detrimental to health, further exacerbating the deleterious health effects of the chronic stress associated with racial discrimination. [16]

As a form of resistance, there is a growing segment of Black women, on social media and in academia, who are pushing back against the "Strong Black Woman" albatross. Tricia Hersey, performance artist and community activist, is the founder of The Nap Ministry, a movement that evangelizes the "liberatory power of rest"[17]:

> Black women, in particular, have been fed this superwoman narrative that says we can do it all. And we love to think that and feel good [about] that. But we've been tricked into believing that lie . . . Even our parents have been teaching us that you have to get up and work hard. That you're lazy if you sleep past a certain time. Keep going! Go, go, go!

Your teachers, your bosses, the church are all part of grind culture. Being told that rest is something that you can't do is a form of violence. [Violence against Black people] is not just about things like police pulling us over and killing us. When you slowly begin to understand that, then you begin to have grace for yourself, you start being soft with yourself. You understand rest as your divine right as a human being.[18]

Hersey, who coined the concepts "rest is resistance" and "rest as reparations," is more than advocating for naps. Her activism is "deeply political work that is disrupting toxic systems."[19]

The research is clear: the notion of the "Strong Black Woman" can be harmful to Black women. The work that Hersey is doing is essential to informing Black women that they have a right to rest. But I believe it is a mistake to negate the strength of Black women or to say Black women are weak.

Forged in the battle for our humanity, strength is our legacy, passed down from one Black woman to another over centuries. Strength does not imply an imperviousness to weakness or weariness. I believe we should reframe the understanding of the "Strong Black Woman" by owning and celebrating a strength that affirms our humanity, prioritizes our health and well-being, establishes boundaries, and asks for help.

My sister shared with me that whenever she is going through a difficult, seemingly impossible circumstance, my grandmother will say to her, "Now don't forget, my blood is running through your veins, and that means you are strong too." My grandmother doesn't say this to shame her granddaughter, but to encourage her. Black women *are* strong, not because they can do it all, but because in the face of obstacles, and the realities of fallibility, they continue to persist.

My experience with my grandmother is not singular. It is the kind of wisdom Black women in the United States have imparted to their daughters, sisters, nieces, cousins, grand-daughters, and so on, for centuries. It is an element of the *secret sauce* that has enabled millions of Black women in the United States to do the seemingly impossible: LIVE.

CREATIVITY

The Black women's inner knowing about other Black women is collective in how it values and reveres Black women. But there is also an inner knowing that is particular to individual Black women, to their personal circumstances and lived experiences.

Alisha Gordon, the Georgia native introduced in chapter one, described her personal inner knowing of Black women in Promethean terms. "We are the most innovative creatures on earth. When you think about innovation, especially in this twenty-first century context of finances and technology . . . when you think about the origins of mankind and all of culture, across the diaspora . . . Black women have a key role in innovating around new ways of thinking [that have] changed the trajectory of political, religious, and corporate spaces."[20] Gordon's perception of Black women as creative and innovative forces is shaped by an understanding of history and the ingenuity of single motherhood. To care for her daughter, Gordon used resourceful methods that stretched a dollar and supplemented her income.

The creativity of Black women is often framed as an extension of survival; about making something out of nothing, making do with what you have. But it is also about art, a reflection of a soul, an expression of beauty within. In the 1972 nonfiction essay, "In Search of Our Mother's Gardens," acclaimed writer, poet, and activist Alice Walker pondered the tragic origins of the Black woman's artistry in the United States.

How was the creativity of the black woman kept alive, year after year and century after century, when for most of the years black people have been in America, it was a punishable crime for a black person to read or write? And the freedom to paint, to sculpt, to expand the mind with action did not exist. Consider, if you can bear to imagine it, what might have been the result if singing, too, had been forbidden by law. Listen to the voices of Bessie Smith, Billie Holiday, Nina Simone, Roberta Flack, and Aretha Franklin, among others, and imagine those voices muzzled for life . . . The agony of the lives of women who might have been Poets, Novelists, Essayists, and Short-Story Writers (over a period of centuries), who died with their real gifts stifled within them.[21]

It is heartbreaking to imagine. Centuries of enslavement stifling creative pursuits of our foremothers. I've often wondered why so many Black women today are subsumed by creativity. From fashion and hairstyling to cooking, baking, writing, singing, dancing, acting, quilting, and so on; creative expression is intertwined with and indistinguishable from Black woman*ness*. I submit that the gifts of our foremothers have not been eradicated but live on in future generations. The creative genius of Black women today is a birthright, an inheritance.

Walker's essay culminated in the realization that her mother had inherited a "vibrant creative spirit."[22] Born early in the twentieth century, Walker's mother married young, had eight children, and "during the 'working' day, she labored beside—not behind"[23]—Walker's father in the fields. It was well into adulthood before Walker noticed that her late mother's garden was actually art, "a garden so brilliant with colors, so original in its design, so magnificent with life and creativity, that to this day people drive by our house in Georgia—perfect strangers and imperfect strangers—and ask to stand or walk among my mother's art . . . I notice that it is only when my mother is working in her flowers that she is radiant."[24] Walker's realization helped me to see that what I took for commonplace domesticity was the embodiment of artist expression.

Simply put: my mom can burn. I mean this in the "down home, southern, made from scratch" kinda way. Flaky biscuits served piping hot, split by a melting pat of butter, crispy golden fried chicken, cheddar (extra-sharp only!) baked macaroni and cheese, collards from the garden, and melt-in-your-mouth caramel cake.

In the early 1950s, my mother's parents moved from Georgia to the Northeast, after a friend secured a job for my grandfather at a firearms manufacturer. They became a part of the Great Migration—the movement of six million Black people from the rural south to cities in the North, Midwest, and West. Like many transplants, every summer my grandparents packed up eight of their nine children and drove "home," so they could connect with their roots and more importantly, stay out of trouble (my grandfather believed the city was too wild for kids). For them, going "home" meant driving seventeen or more hours to the family farm in Sumter County, Georgia. It was during those hot summers that my maternal great-grandmother, Meta Bell Kearse, taught my mom the techniques of southern cooking—cultivating the next generation of great cooks and bakers.

My mother's culinary skills, like the garden tended by Walker's mother, won praise and acclaim. When I was a child, everybody said my mom could out-cook and bake anyone. Some of my fondest memories are of her teaching (just like she was taught) my sisters and me how to cook "by sight"—that is cooking with intuition, without using a measuring cup. "See how this looks?" she would say. "When you see those air bubbles, it means it's time to add a bit more of this or a pinch of that." She taught her daughters every trick of the cooking trade but fiercely guarded familial trade secrets.

I recall one of my mother's friends scooping me onto her lap, my baby-girl legs dangling off to one side as she pulled me close and whispered, "What does your mommy put in the filling of her pineapple cake, honey? You can tell me!" And with the discretion of a young child reveling in attention, I shamelessly spilled my guts, "Milk, sugar, eggs!" Thankfully I was completely wrong and nothing I shared was proprietary. But even if I had told it all, my mom knew it didn't matter; "some foods taste better," she has always explained, "not because of the ingredients, but how and when you add the ingredients. That makes all the difference in the world—that, in and of itself, is a secret." In other words, even when my mom shared a recipe, it rarely tasted like she made it.

Many years ago, Meta Bell told my mother that she had the "gift of cooking." It was the highest compliment that any cook in our family could receive. My great-grandmother recognized her granddaughter's artistry. An art that brought my mom and others joy.

Walker admitted that her mother's life was "so hindered and intruded upon in so many ways,"[25] yet being an artist had "still been a daily part of her life. This ability to hold on, even in very simple ways, is work black women have done for a very long time."[26] As a source of freedom, joy, independence, and strength, creativity is a special ingredient of the *secret sauce*.

FAITH

In 1979 in northeastern Indiana, the mall bustled with activity and seasonal cheer. As shoppers searched for the perfect

Christmas gifts, holiday decorations and colorful lights hung from store windows.

Susie Mitchell walked slowly, desultorily through the local mall. She wasn't there to shop, but she just didn't know what else to do. Held tightly against her body, balanced on one hip, she carried her eleven-month-old son.

At twenty-five, she was married, owned a home, had a beautiful baby boy, was the first Black employee to work at the local credit union, and, a few years earlier, had travelled to Paris and London as part of a one-year business program. A casual observer might assume Mitchell was living the dream, but she was isolated, alone, and desperately unhappy. Her husband was physically abusive, and he cheated on her with other women.

Mitchell knew her husband in high school and reconnected with him a year after graduation. They began dating, but Mitchell had reservations about taking the next step because she knew he liked to party, do drugs, and hang out. But she was feeling pressured, "everybody back then was like, so when you gonna get married? [At the time] I was twenty-three and by then you'd think I was an old maid . . . Everybody in the group got married, so we got married [too] . . . I knew I shouldn't have married him, but I married him anyway."[27] Nearly three years later—hopeless, depressed, and suicidal—Mitchell deeply regretted her decision.

That night, as she walked through the mall with her young son in her arms, she came upon a group singing Christmas carols and she stopped to listen. "Those people, they were singing, and they looked so happy and at that point I was trying to get my happiness from my son because that's all I had."[28]

One of the women singing noticed Mitchell. She stepped away from the choir and walked toward the young mother. Mitchell instantly recognized the woman as her Sunday school teacher from her childhood church. Delighted to see a friendly, familiar face, Mitchell recounted that "she sat down, and she started talking to me . . . And it was like she knew everything I was doing, but she talked to me with such love. And, then she invited me to church."[29]

In the first week of the new year, on the first Sunday in 1980, Mitchell visited her friend's church, "Fifty people got saved that Sunday, from one end of the hall to the other end of it. The reverend prayed for each one of us and prayed specifically and you knew it was the Lord . . . and I got saved."[30]

For nearly a decade following the encounter at the mall, Mitchell's tumultuous marriage was defined by a dizzying seesaw of separation and reconciliation and the birth of two more children. It was a chaotic, traumatic period. Mitchell lived in constant fear of her angry and erratic husband. But she was thankful she no longer had to face her problems alone.

> I slept with forks in all my windows so I would hear if he would try to come in. [One night], I had the kids. I am in the house, and I hear him unscrew the deadbolt off my front door. I laid there in that bed, [but I didn't get up]. I said, "Lord I am not gonna live like this for the rest of my life, either you real or you ain't, either you going to protect me or you're not, but I'm not going to live like this." And after he unscrewed the deadbolt, the door didn't open, it just wouldn't open. From that day forward I was never afraid because I knew that God was real.[31]

Mitchell believed God had miraculously kept the door from opening. And that incident gave her the courage to file for legal separation and eventually divorce. When her father asked how she was going to raise three children by herself, she told him, "me and Jesus, Jesus and me."[32]

Aided by the love and support of her church family, Mitchell completely rebuilt her life. Several years later, after six months of dating, Mitchell married a kind, gentle, and Godly man. After more than thirty years of marriage, Mitchell remains thankful, "It's like Lord I can't forget what you've done."[33]

* * *

I come from a long lineage of faith. I am a Christian, raised in a Christian household. I have literally been going to church since I was in my mother's womb. In fact, my father is a pastor, my mother calls herself the "hand-maiden of the Lord," and for years my older sister worked for a church as the praise and worship coordinator. Just about everyone in my extended family, on both sides, are Christians.

My late maternal grandmother, Elnora Wright Kearse, helped to establish Mount Moriah Baptist Church in Hartford, Connecticut, in the 1950s. My paternal great-grandfather, Sidney Thurmond, was described in his obituary as "a believer in hard work, and an even greater believer in God."[34] He is quoted in the obituary as saying often, "Everything I put my hands on He made a success. God has been with me all the way up the road."[35] I have two uncles who are pastors (as well as their wives), one aunt who is an evangelist, and several aunts and uncles who have been deacons at some time or another. This list does not include cousins—once, twice, or even thrice removed—who serve in the church in some official or lay capacity.

While it is important to acknowledge my Christian-based perspective and lens, it is even more important to understand that my analysis is not based on personal beliefs. It is grounded in existing research and the exclusive national survey of Black women I conducted in partnership with the Marist Poll.

In 2021, the Pew Research Center published a survey that exclusively explored faith among Black Americans. The survey found "about three-quarters of Black Americans (74 percent) believe in God 'as described in the Bible'"[36] and are generally more religious than Americans overall. A consumer report conducted by the Nielsen Company in 2017 found that 83 percent of Black women consider themselves spiritual people and 62 percent say they attend religious services regularly.[37] When Black women were asked in 2012, in a national survey run by the *Washington Post* and the Kaiser Family Foundation, how important a role faith played during times of turmoil, "87 percent of black women— much more than any other group—say they turn to their faith to get through."[38] The survey of Black women I conducted with the Marist Poll in 2021 found similar trends. When asked how much guidance religion provides in their day-to-day lives, nearly all Black women (99 percent) say it provides at least some level of guidance. Given the overwhelming data, it is fair to postulate that Black women are the most deeply religious or spiritual group in the United States—an important source of strength and comfort.

An emerging trend among Black women is the growing number practicing African spirituality, like the Yoruba, Hoodoo, and Conjuring traditions. Dr. Yvonne Chireau is a professor at Swarthmore College and the author of *Black Magic: Religion and the African American Conjuring Tradition*. At a Harvard Divinity School event highlighting her work, Chireau explained:

> Today's practitioners of hoodoo are predominantly, and again, I have to do some study on this, predominantly Black women. They share a unifying principle in their belief that ancestral spirituality is foundational to community heal- ing . . . not just the healing of bodies, but the healing of relationships—connecting, restoring, and strengthening

relationships between those who came before, those who are present now, between the dead and the living, between the natural realm and the social world in which all humanity moves.[39]

For many of the Black women exploring ancestral spirituality, "healing often comes in the form of liberation and resistance . . . in a time when America's racist foundation has been pushed to the foreground, seeking solace in this connection feels especially poignant."[40] These African traditions offer some Black women a way to practice a faith that honors their roots and ancestors.

Similar to the overall population, the religious landscape for Black folks is evolving, particularly among younger generations. Based on a survey from the Pew Research Center, about one in five Black Americans (21 percent) are not affiliated with any religion. This religiously unaffiliated category (sometimes called religious "nones") includes those who describe themselves as atheist, agnostic, or "nothing in particular" when asked about their religion. About half of Black religious "nones" say they believe in reincarnation and a little more than a third believe that prayers to ancestors can protect them from harm. It is a shift reflected in the Marist Poll results. Even though nearly all Black women say religion provides guidance in their day-to-day lives, for older generations, the degree of that guidance is greater—50 percent of Baby Boomers believe religion provides a great deal of guidance, while just 30 percent of Gen Z/Millennials feel the same way.

Candice Marie Benbow is a theologian and author of *Red Lip Theology: For Church Girls Who've Considered Tithing to the Beauty Supply Store When Sunday Morning Isn't Enough.* Benbow grew up in a Black Missionary Baptist Church in North Carolina. Raised by a single mother, Christianity was central to Benbow's formative years.

But experiences in college, seminary, and the untimely death of her mother had a profound impact on Benbow's belief system. She wrote that she grew increasingly disillusioned with Christianity. Influenced by womanist and Black liberation theology and exhausted by "the patriarchal presence within Black spaces,"[41] Benbow stopped attending church services regularly and embarked on a two-year spiritual exploration, free from the constraints of the Black Church.

> I joined a Buddhist community and attended their weekly gatherings. I studied African traditional religions and ways to listen for the voices of the ancestors, the orishas, and Spirit—seeking my true spiritual home. I read women's spiritual autobiographies, beginning with Sue Monk Kidd's *The Dance of the Dissident Daughter*. And what I learned is Spirit is everywhere, and the fluidity of the Divine only adds to its beauty. Equally, I was learning to trust the sound of the feminine in the spiritual space.[42]

In her book, Benbow articulated a new, personal theology "grounded in the teachings of Jesus, the wisdom of the ancestors, and the power of Black womanhood."

Larger numbers of Black women are experimenting and expanding the scope of their faith and spiritual practices. Some have rejected Christianity in lieu of African traditions, others like Benbow are choosing to amalgamize a range of beliefs to create something new, and then there are those, like me, who have chosen to remain in the Christian faith. Although spiritual and faith practices are rapidly evolving, they are likely to continue to be an important source of grounding and strength for Black women for the foreseeable future.

SISTERHOOD

The warm sound of full-throated laughter filled the air. Eyes glistened with joy. On a recent summer evening at home, four longtime friends sat close, elbows touching each time one of them leaned in for a bite. Intimate comradery cultivated by nearly five decades of proven trust and steadfast love.

In the 1950s, Laura Green, Angela Brady, Diretha Franklin, and Ruth Grayer were each born in northeastern Ohio. In the latter half of the twentieth century, they each married young, worked and raised their families in Rust-Belt communities devastated by deindustrialization, population decline, and poverty. I met them nearly a decade ago while visiting friends in the Midwestern state, and I've always admired their sisterhood.

During the 1980s, they each joined the Church at Warren Healing and Learning Center, a full gospel, nondenominational church in Cortland. Deeply devoted to their faith, they were involved in church ministry, including vacation Bible school, cleaning the sanctuary on Saturdays, prison ministry, and attending overnight women's retreats. Time spent worshiping and servicing at church solidified their friendships. They are quick to point out that, while their personalities and tastes are distinct, they are bound by a shared faith and common journey.

Green is often called "Sister Love" because of her loving nature and persistent acts of kindness. Franklin brings her wisdom and strength to the group, someone each woman has turned to for advice, support, and encouragement over the years. Grayer, a fireball of energy, is known for her infectious joy and laughter. And Brady is considered the role model "with the picket fence," due to her long marriage, calming demeanor, and soft-spoken voice.

These fabulous four women call themselves "the Kenilworth Crew," an ode to Kenilworth Avenue in Warren, Ohio, where each of them lived concurrently in the late 1980s. "Laura and Angie lived behind each other," explains Franklin, "and me and Laura lived across the street, and Ruth lived on the other side of Kenilworth."[43] By this time, Green, Franklin, and Grayer had divorced their first husbands and were raising their children as single mothers, a burden Green says was eased by their friendship and support.

> You know when you're single and you're going through things, and you just got to hold on? So, I would call Diretha at two o'clock in the morning and she would talk me through until I was strong . . . We helped each other, we would say "you need toilet paper? Meet me under the streetlight." That's how close we were. If I don't got it, they got it; if they got it, we all got it. If the gas man was coming, we would call and say the gas man is coming, or the water man is coming to turn our water off.[44]

Franklin fondly recounted group trips to Mosquito Lake State Park with their children: "We would go to the lake, and this is what we would do. What would ask each other, what do you have? And we would bring what we have and put it together and we'd have a nice picnic . . . we'd have a good time and sit on a blanket and talk. And we encouraged each other."[45]

Green, Franklin, and Grayer were also connected by a shared life experience and new worldview. Each of them had difficult, unhappy first marriages, and now they were only interested in getting remarried if it was God's will for their lives. Green remembers how important their friendships were during those years: "We kept encouraging each other, 'Girl we just got to hang in there, God's got a husband for you . . . we're waiting for what God is going to send us.'"[46]

Their faith worked. In the span of four years, starting with Grayer in 1987, Rodgers in 1989, and Franklin in 1991, all three women married amazing, wonderful men they met at church.

Over the years, their friendships helped them maintain their faith in God, raise their children and grandchildren, and weather the storms of life.

> We know each other, we know our stories, we encourage one another, we can get mad at one another, but we don't stay mad . . . We go back too far, I know that no matter what, at the end of the day they gon be there, and we gon be there for each other, even though we have weakness, even though we make each other mad, even though our kids may be at each other, it's like ya'll know, don't forget where you came from.[47]

Agreeing with Green, Brady sees their friendship as "providential, I feel like they are a gift," her voice trailed off and her eyes filled up with tears before continuing, "from God."[48] This prompted Green, Grayer, and Franklin to say unanimously, "aww, we feel the same way!"[49]

Sisterhood, the bond exhibited between the Kenilworth Crew, is a key element of Black women's *secret sauce* and informs how they "get over." It reinforces value, serving as a buffer between a world that demonizes, fetishizes, and demeans Black womanhood.

In a peer-reviewed paper appearing in the *Journal of Black Psychology* in 2004, Dr. Kelly Patterson examined the self-esteem of Black women from 1979–1992 using data from the National Survey of Black Americans (NSBA). The study was remarkable for the transformative ways in which it presented Black women.

First, it challenged the idea that Black women are "predicted to have low self-esteem because scholars thought they internalized demeaning messages of themselves and measured themselves against a [w]hite female standard. Since they could never live up to the white 'ideal,' it was surmised that they would not value themselves."[50] Dr. Patterson's fresh analysis of the NSBA survey revealed that Black women in the study had high levels of self-esteem and were able to maintain that high level over a fourteen-year period.

Second, the study found that "Black women are the primary source of Black women's self-esteem because it is their evaluations that are most important for their own self-assessments. Black women validate the experience, perspective, and feelings of African American women that mainstream society attempts to invalidate."[51]

And third, the paper highlighted "the deliberate process of building the self-esteem of community members—particularly young Black girls. This process was necessary more than a century ago to give young slave girls dignity in the face of inhumanity, and it endures today as members of African American women's support networks seek to build their self-worth in a society that devalues them."[52]

This sense of self-worth that is formed and buttressed by Black women sisterhood is echoed in the Marist Poll findings. We found that 80 percent of Black women agree with the statement that they see themselves as someone who has high self-esteem, and nearly eight in ten (78 percent) agree that Black women are part of a sisterhood.

Despite ethnographic narratives and research findings that validate the sisterhood, a quote "all my skinfolk ain't kinfolk" (attributed to and popularized by anthropologist, writer, and folklorist Zora Neale Hurston) challenges the veracity and strength of the sisterhood. In this context, the warning is clear, shared identity does not connote solidarity or fidelity.

The quote points to a deeply ingrained, long-standing notion within the Black community that Black women do not help or support one another, particularly when it comes to upward mobility. This so-called rivalry between Black women is due in part to a perception that there are a limited number of seats at the proverbial table of power. Taken at face value, coupled with stories I've heard and my own observations, these interactions are demoralizing and present significant impediments to sisterhood. But I take issue with a narrative that paints a broad brush of competition and division between Black women.

First, it implies that there is something unusual or deviant about Black women not getting along. As humans, Black women can and will experience the full range of emotions and feelings during intragroup interactions.

Second, the idea of rivalry promulgates scarcity, a tool of oppression. Scarcity is a mindset, a way of looking at the world that can be traced back to the enslavement of Africans. Enslaved people literally had to eat the crumbs from the master's table. Those crumbs are analogous to the modern-day seat of power, the master's table is analogous to the modern-day table of power and the master then and now, generally speaking, is white people. This historical analogy fuels the notion that there is not enough room for those who are not white men. But the data presented in this book prove that where Black women were, is not where Black women are now. If there is enough sky for an infinite number of stars, then there *is* enough room for all Black women to flourish.

And third, the prevalence of these stories serves to silence stories of Black women supporting, uplifting Black women.

After nearly six years combined in college and graduate school and another twenty-plus years in the workforce, I can think of only ONE Black woman I thought was intentionally trying to sabotage my progress and dampen my shine. But I have dozens of stories of Black women, especially during my decade at CBS News—Debbie Mitchell, Debbye Turner Bell, Anjie Taylor, Rene Syler, Paulette Brown, Crystal Johns, Erika Wortham, Aurelia Grayson, Cathy Black, and more—who were my sisters. These women taught me to be a better producer, journalist, and writer, held me close when my sister unexpectedly died, offered career advice, and listened to me complain about promotions I thought took too long to come to fruition. I thrived in the harsh competitive world of broadcast network news because Black women stood by me, had my back, encouraged me, and celebrated every success. There was no jealousy or back-stabbing— only the bonds of sisterhood.

I firmly believe that more often than not, Black women can count on the solidarity of the sisterhood. It is our legacy. It is the reason I can walk into a room or store or any public space, and invariably connect with the only other Black woman in the room. We'll lock eyes, nod knowingly, and say, "I got you girl," without uttering one word.

Black women's foremothers, creativity, faith, and sisterhood make up the *secret sauce*. It is how they do what they do, and it has led to the creation of their own ethos: take the bitter, add the sweet, and create a powerful way of living.

CHAPTER 3
LEMONADE LIFESTYLE

I called my mom one afternoon and said, "I can't remember, what is our family recipe for lemonade?"

"Why?" she asked, laughing. I couldn't help but smile. We both knew she was in heaven. She loves it when I ask for advice—it's proof I still need her. Which of course I do, especially when it comes to cooking. As our laughter subsided, my mom rattled off Meta Bell's, my great-grandmother's, simple, yet elegant lemonade recipe. A lesson passed down from grandmother to granddaughter sixty years ago:

Place a metal two-quart-sized pitcher into the deep freezer overnight. The next morning, add one cup of sugar, two lemons (that have been squeezed and diced) and one cup of cold water to the pitcher. Repeat, until six lemons are used. Stir mixture with a wooden spoon. Prepare six washed-out canning glasses with ice cubes. Garnish each glass with a thin slice of lemon. Serve and relax as you cool off.

As a child, I despised lemonade. Lemons were just too bitter to consume in any form. But now, I can appreciate the intermix of bitter and sweet, my taste buds and maturity having evolved synchronously.

The making of lemonade portends an optimistic *weltanschauung*, "when life gives you lemons, make lemonade." This is often understood to mean, "Stay positive regardless of shitty circumstances!" or, "Look for opportunities in misfortune!" But I believe the proverb is more nuanced than these pedestrian interpretations suggest. It means more than passively coping, belatedly reacting, or wistfully wishing for circumstances to change.

Making lemonade is a lifestyle. It is analogous to a formula, a methodology for living with intention, marked by courage, agency, and audacity. I posit that Black women in the United States who have realized their personal definition of success—whether starting a business, raising a family, or climbing Mount Kilimanjaro—have achieved a Lemonade Lifestyle that is generational in the making. A lifestyle that has been shaped and honed by Black women since the earliest enslaved Africans were forcibly brought to the English colonies in 1619. Scholars have uncovered the names of at least two of those African women among the first to arrive: Isabella and Angela.

Isabella arrived near land that later became Hampton, Virginia, on August 25, 1619, and was purchased by Captain William Tucker. In 1623, Isabella had a child with Antony, another enslaved African. Their son, William Tucker, "became the first documented African child born in English-occupied North America."[1] More than a decade later they "gained their freedom . . . and started a homestead in Kent County, Virginia."[2] Angela is listed in the 1624 and 1625 census as living in the household of Captain William Pierce, a well-connected, wealthy planter-merchant who was married to a woman named Joan.

Historians believe Angela "was likely enslaved, not indentured"[3] and worked alongside her mistress growing "figs," raising "hogs," and "keeping house."[4]

Four hundred years later, the Lemonade Lifestyle has helped Black women continuously press for the freedom and right to live life on their own terms. Though lemonade is a universal drink, and many people globally have their own cultural articulations of how to make it, there is a particular nuance of multigenerational southern lemonade making that has passed through Black womanhood which defines this particular theory.

Like the metal pitcher my great-grandmother placed in the deep freezer overnight to ensure an optimal temperature the following day, the Lemonade Lifestyle begins with investing the time to develop purpose and perseverance. Lemons represent the universal hardships of life. But for Black women, lemons also comprise the bitter taste of intersectional oppressions and structural inequality. Sugar is exemplified by the *secret sauce* engendering a sweet strength that enables Black women to face adversity and strive toward a future of their own making. This lemonade, a Black women's lemonade, is subsumed by love, hope, and imagination. And like the tide of an ocean, the Lemonade Lifestyle ebbs and flows, rises and falls, retreats and advances. Learning to ride that wave is essential.

To demand the right to live free is engagement in war. To battle is to accept the inevitability of loss and defeat. To battle is hope. The hope that efforts will effectuate a better tomorrow. To accept the status quo is failure. The Lemonade Lifestyle is not an easy path of least resistance. The potential costs are high: burnout, weariness, disappointment. But living the Lemonade Lifestyle is moving forward—the actualization of self-respect, agency, and power.

Agnéz Deréon was a Black, French-speaking Creole from Louisiana born in the early 1900s. Like Meta Bell's descendants, her progeny are the grateful beneficiaries of a lemonade recipe:

> Take one pint of water. Add a half-pound of sugar, the juice of eight lemons, and the zest of half of a lemon. Pour the water from one jug into the other several times, strain through a clean napkin.[5]

This is the recipe one of her granddaughters, Beyoncé Knowles-Carter, shared on her sixth solo album, aptly named *Lemonade*. Presented visually, *Lemonade* is largely about infidelity and its devastating consequences, but it is also an archetype of the Lemonade Lifestyle.

The tenth track, "Freedom," is an empowering anthem showcasing Beyoncé's *puissance*. The lyrics affirm that lemons (or Jay Z's cheatin' ass) will not be her undoing: "Cause a winner don't quit on themselves."[6] The song culminates with an audio clip of Jay Z's grandmother, Hattie White, speaking at her ninetieth birthday party in 2015. "I had my ups and downs," Smith admits with the dignity of an elder, "but I always find the inner strength to pull myself up. I was served lemons, but I made lemonade."[7]

Dr. Kinitra Brooks is a scholar of Beyoncé's *Lemonade*. An English professor at Michigan State University with an expertise in the study of Black women, genre fiction, and popular culture, Brooks earned national attention for creating one of the first courses to examine *Lemonade* in the academe. Entitled *Black Women, Beyoncé and Popular Culture,* the course used "*Lemonade* as a starting point to examine the sociocultural issues that are most prominent in black womanhood through black feminist theory, literature, music, and film."[8]

Brooks is also the co-editor of the book *The Lemonade Reader*, "an anthology of essays, ideas and 'interludes' inspired by both *Lemonade* and Beyoncé, written by predominantly Black female academics, pop cultural critics and activists."[9] In an interview with me one afternoon, Brooks spoke of the importance of Beyoncé's *Lemonade* to the academic discourse and its timeless relevance with regard to the lived experiences of Black women:

> What it offers is a blueprint. A lot of people talked about Jay Z's album, *The Blueprint*, but *Lemonade* offers a blueprint on how to find peace, self-love, and self-expression as a Black woman and how to weather the storm. She provides quite a few themes. She's saying, 'go home,' she goes home to her mother's people in western Louisiana; 'go near' water because water is life giving and water is also a way in which we realize that there are things out there that are bigger than us; and commune with your elders and ancestors, that there is knowledge that they have that they can impart to us.[10]

For Brooks, Beyoncé made a calculated decision to make an album that elevated, celebrated, and honored the lived experiences of Black women.

Beyoncé may be, in the words of *Harper's BAZAAR*, "a cultural force who has routinely defied expectations and transformed the way we understand the power of art to change how we see ourselves and each other,"[11] but her massive celebrity and wealth do not bestow an aptitude for living the Lemonade Lifestyle. There is no special dispensation that enables Beyoncé to be a "winner"[12] who "breaks chains all by herself."[13] As a Black woman in the United States, Beyoncé's resilience is largely due to the legacy of Black woman*ness*. The inspiration, the strength underpinning *Lemonade*, originates with our foremothers. The Lemonade Lifestyle is for *all* Black women, including me.

* * *

When I was six years old, I asked my father if I was going to die.

I am in his arms, and he is running.

It is the summer of 1985. Sunday afternoon. My father's thirty-sixth birthday. I feel happy and pretty in my crinoline slip, which I keep on after slipping out of my church dress. I am twirling and singing to myself as little girls do. I dance into our small kitchen.

My mom is frying chicken. My older sister stands on a chair at the sink washing dishes. I hear something. Turning around I see hot cooking oil slide down the stove and onto the floor. I walk backwards into the wall. I have nowhere else to go. I slip on the fiery oil, falling to my knees.

My sister screams—pleads with me to get on a chair. My mother is frozen, rendered mute and immobile. I feel bewildered, confused. I only think of escaping the searing pain, so I begin to crawl through the hot oil. My dad hears my screams. He rushes out of his bedroom, picks me up and runs outside towards our tan Ford station wagon.

"No, baby, you are not going to die."

As we drive the short distance to the hospital, my dad's words comfort me. And I believe him.

* * *

Nearly forty years have passed since that fateful summer day. Now the scars have become old, familiar friends. Eyes closed and palms face down, I sometimes trace my bumpy skin: toes to thighs, thighs to toes.

Third-degree burns destroyed layers of my skin, irrevocably damaging hair follicles, sweat glands, and underlying tissue.
In short, my legs were irreparably scarred. In the months following the near-fatal accident, doctors shared with my parents that
I would never be "normal."

I would never ride a bike, run, or walk properly. I would
never eat fried foods because hot cooking oil would remind me
of the accident. My prospects, from mobility to marriage (one
elementary classmate told me that my legs were so ugly, no one
would ever want to marry me) were dismal.

Ashes beget beauty.

Mourning begets joy.

And scars beget victory.

But my parents purchased a bike for me anyway and I've
been riding since the accident. In high school, following the
example of my older sister, I became a cheerleader, which meant
I was considerably more active than the doctors had anticipated.
And perhaps more importantly, I have always loved to cook.
And I really enjoy a good piece of fried chicken. My grade school
classmate was wrong too: I've had my share of boyfriends, and
not one of them has ever cared about my scars.

Admittedly, there was a time when I hid my scars behind
thick, knitted tights—refusing to take them off in public. I
wore them every summer, even in the swimming pool. There
was a time when I struggled to comprehend why. Why had I
been burned? Why did I spend eight years of my childhood
in and out of hospitals undergoing reconstructive surgeries?
Why were my legs permanently scarred? What was the point
of the pain? I could have decided that too many lemons were
stacked against me. That circumstances, beyond my control, had ruined my life. Instead, I learned the power of the
Lemonade Lifestyle.

* * *

If lemonade is a formula for living life well, then its methodol-ogy is a pathway to the American Dream. There is conjecture surrounding the origins of the American Dream. There is also scholarly debate about its original meaning. Does the American Dream still hold import and if so, for whom? And what does it mean in the new millennium?

Social scientists John White and Sandra Hanson describe in their book, *The American Dream in the 21st Century,* that "at its core, the American Dream represents a state of mind . . . and enduring optimism"[14] that enables people to "repeatedly rise from the ashes."[15] It is an idea, they argue, that remains relevant:

> The American Dream is deeply embedded in American mythology and in the consciousness of its citizens. That is exactly what gives the American Dream its staying power, even in times when it seems as though it should surely die. After all, myths last because they are dreams fulfilled in our imaginations. So it is with the American Dream. And because it finds fulfillment either in one's own life or in the lives of others, Americans are ever more devoted to it.[16]

An understanding of the American Dream lies on an ideologi-cal spectrum. On one end, scholars like twentieth century histo-rian James Truslow Adams reasoned that the original concept is much more than the acquisition of wealth and fame:

> It is not a dream of motor cars and high wages merely, but a dream of social order in which each man and each woman shall be able to attain to the fullest stature of which they are innately capable, and be recognized by others for

what they are, regardless of the fortuitous circumstances of their birth . . . It has been a dream of being able to grow to the fullest development as a man and woman . . . [17]

But on the other end, the modern understanding is centered on capitalist ideals of naked individualism and materialism. The Dream, today, as explored by University of London professor Sarah Churchwell, is "a dream of personal opportunity, in which 'opportunity' is gauged primarily in economic terms, and those opportunities are shrinking."[18]

Recently, adults in the United States were asked by researchers what the American Dream meant to them: "By contrast, majorities say 'freedom of choice in how to live' (77 percent), having a good family life (70 percent), and retiring comfortably (60 percent) are essential to their view of the American dream."[19]

Most historians believe the American Dream is rooted in the writings of English philosopher John Locke who wrote that all individuals were born with "inalienable" natural rights such as the "right to life, liberty, and property."[20] At the dawn of a new nation, Thomas Jefferson imbued Locke's philosophy into the Declaration of Independence when he wrote, "We hold these truths to be self-evident, that all men are created equal, that they are endowed by their Creator with certain unalienable Rights, that among these are Life, Liberty, and the pursuit of Happiness."

For me, these three words—life, liberty, and happiness—are at the core of the American Dream. Everyone has the right to live, to breathe, to exist. It should be that simple. But once there is life (and provided one is lawful and respectful of others), there should also be the liberty to make choices for one's own life. And once you are alive and you are free, the right to pursue happiness is itself life-giving. What makes one individual happy is as varied as the grains of sand on the beach. What has been at the center of racial and gendered strife in the United States goes back to the restriction of life, liberty, and pursuit of happiness for millions of African descendants, for Indigenous peoples, and for women.

Historically—at times de jure and at other times de facto—the American Dream has been akin to a "Whites Only" sign posted on the front door of a Jim Crow–era restaurant. An inherent tension, predicated on racially gendered identities. Opportunities rendered elusive.

Still, a Pew Research Center survey published in 2017 found "most Americans say they have achieved the 'American dream' or are on their way to achieving it."[21] While Blacks when compared to whites and Latinos are less likely to say they had achieved the American Dream, Blacks (62 percent) are significantly more likely to say they are on their way to achieving it than Latinos (51 percent) and whites (42 percent). This suggests a heightened level of optimism felt by Black people.

In the summer of 2020, YouGov asked fourteen thousand US adults if they see the American Dream as attainable. While most of those polled—Native Americans (57 percent), white Americans (56 percent), Hispanic Americans (53 percent), Asian Americans (50 percent)—see the American Dream as attainable, just (45 percent) of Black Americans felt the same. In fact, roughly one in six Black Americans (17 percent) say that there is no such thing as the American Dream.[22]

Inequalities exacerbated by the COVID-19 virus and the high-profile police murders of Black people changed the calculus. It is understandable that some Black folks are wary, skeptical, or simply don't believe in the promise of the American Dream. For centuries, they have been locked in a struggle against hate and intolerance.

And while the bleak reality causes many Black and Brown folks to reject the American Dream, I am not one of them.

I have no illusions about this country, her sins, and what and who she is. Afterall, I am a Black woman. Born and bred in the United States. I am aware of who I am and how I am perceived. The vagina between my legs, brown skin stretched across my bones. How perceptions, prejudices, and discrimination serve to limit, to entrap, to ensnare, to hinder the manifestation of my dreams. Despite all that, and maybe because of it, I have the audacity to pursue a Dream that was not intended for me or people who share my blood.

"I am the dream and the hope of the slave,"[23] the revered poet Maya Angelou once wrote. It is hard to imagine a more noble pursuit than to embody the hopes and dreams of our enslaved ancestors. The pursuit of life, liberty, and happiness—the original conceit of the American Dream—is one way to do just that.

Black folks have been at the forefront of pushing the United States—from slave rebellions, *Brown v. Board of Education*, the Civil Rights Act of 1964, the Voting Rights Act of 1965, to the Black Lives Matter Movement—to live up to ideals espoused in its founding documents. Let's also fight for the American Dream.

My perspective is what the first Black US president, Barack Obama, called the audacity of hope: "The audacity to believe despite all the evidence to the contrary . . . the gall to believe that despite personal setbacks, the loss of a job or an illness in the family or a childhood mired in poverty, we had some control—and therefore responsibility—over our own fate."[24] I place Black women in the center of the American Dream. For we are her greatest exemplar. Consider Dr. Constance Citro's analysis of census data for this book, which showed Black women's high rate of growth over an eighty-year[25] period—particularly in real median wages (adjusted for inflation) and the completion of four years or more of college—saw the biggest percentage increase of all four sex/race groups examined.

Also consider the national survey of Black women I did in partnership with the Marist Poll. When Black women were asked whether success in life is pretty much determined by forces outside of their control or if everyone has it in their own power to succeed, three in four Black women (75 percent) believe that everyone has it in their own power to succeed, whereas 25 percent believe success is determined by outside forces.

This survey contradicts the negative normative conceptions found in the media and in academia that consistently link Black women to lack. Not only do most Black women (70 percent) say they are successful, but they know their success is made possible because of the choices they have made, despite circumstances and structural oppression.

* * *

More Black women (17 percent) are in the process of starting or running new businesses than white men (15 percent) or white women (10 percent)—this is according to *Harvard Business Review* (*HBR*) research done in partnership with the Global Entrepreneurship Monitor's most recent annual survey.[26] But the positive results presented are nullified by the article's introduction: "Despite starting businesses at a high rate, [just] 3 percent of Black women are running mature businesses. In contrast, white women are more than twice as likely to be mature business owners."[27]

The *HBR* report goes on to list "possible reasons Black women entrepreneurs struggle to sustain their businesses."[28]

Explanations include types of businesses started, access to capital, and the uneven distribution of key resources needed for entrepreneurship. While the article acknowledged that "Black women are positioned to play an increasingly visible and important role in the United States' political and economic future,"[29] it ascribes the success of Black women entrepreneurs to the whims, the action, or inaction of others:

> This dream will not be complete without targeted efforts that enable Black women entrepreneurs to grow and sustain their businesses. This will require conscious efforts by the government and private sector to uncover and address gaps and biases in entrepreneurial ecosystems in a way that provides inclusivity and support for the diversity of entrepreneurs that bring economic and social value to American society.[30]

While businesses, governments, and people with resources should support a diverse community of entrepreneurs, I can attest that Black women do what it takes to make a way—waiting for someone to do something is not our modus vivendi. It is important to acknowledge the agency of Black women, that we are active participants in our own fates.

Venture capital funds are increasingly becoming an essential component of successful new businesses. Recent data from Crunchbase (accounting for the first half of 2021) found "startups with at least one Black woman as a founder have raised around $494 million so far in 2021, already surpassing the $484 million raised in all of 2018, the previous five-year high."[31] As wonderful as this sounds, it is a small slice of the VC pie: "Black female startup founders raised just 0.34 percent"[32] of the record $322.8 billion invested by venture capitalists in the United States in 2021. In recent years, a growing number of Black women–led startups crossed the $1 million threshold but "the majority of Black women–led startups raise[d] significantly less than the average funded startup. For those who have not raised over $1 million, the median seed round raised by Black women founders was $125,000 . . . [yet] the national median seed round funding for a startup was $2.5M."[33]

The small percentage of VC dollars raised by Black women has resulted in subpar financial support and many struggle to grow and sustain mature businesses. As a result, as shown in the aforementioned HBR study, "61 percent of Black women self-fund their total startup capital.[34]

Adding to the challenges faced by Black folks is historically lower earning power and data that shows they "take on a higher level of debt to go to college and are less likely to own their own home."[35] The impact to Black entrepreneurs, particularly Black women, is real and frustrating.

The picture is clear; formidable impediments stand in opposition to the success of Black women entrepreneurs. But *how* Black women continue to push for advancement is an illustration of the Lemonade Lifestyle.

It was 2015, and Arlan Hamilton was homeless and living at the San Francisco airport. She was in her mid-thirties—Black, queer, without capital or a college degree—but she had a dream to create her own VC firm after failing to "convince existing venture capital firms to invest in companies led by women, people of color, and LGBT[Q] founders."[36]

Hamilton faced daunting barriers, yet every day for five months, she "took her suitcase and boarded an airport shuttle to Palo Alto or Mountain View California. There she doggedly pursued investors, inviting them to invest in her fund. 'These were not formal meetings,' she clarified. 'A lot of it was me walking side-by-side with them as they walked out of something, or away from something, or away from me.'"[37]

Ultimately, Hamilton secured funding and launched her own venture capital fund, Backstage Capital. Since 2015, Backstage Capital has invested in more than two hundred companies led by underrepresented founders (women, People of Color, and LGBTQ2+). In 2018, Hamilton announced a new $36 million fund[38] that would invest exclusively in Black women founders, $1 million at a time. "They're calling it a 'diversity fund,'" Hamilton wrote in a tweet at the time, but, "I'm calling it an IT'S ABOUT DAMN TIME fund."[39]

In the summer of 2022, Hamilton announced on her podcast, "Your First Million," that Backstage Capital had laid off the majority of its staff. This news came a few months after the firm had "narrowed its investment strategy to only participate in follow-on rounds of existing portfolios."[40] During the podcast, Hamilton admitted that "it has been a depressing, deflating time."[41] But she explained that she did not "feel like there's any sort of failure on the fund side, on the firm's side, on Backstage's side, it's that this could have been avoided if systems were different, if the system we work within were different."[42]

Hamilton's intended audience for the podcast were Backstage Capital stakeholders and community members. She took the time to explain in detail what was happening and to whom, why she made certain decisions, and to assure them that she was committed to the success of the firm. By the end of the twenty-minute podcast, Hamilton seemed certain of three things: she needed rest and would be taking time to take care of herself so she could continue to work and invest in others; she wanted joy, fun, and happinesses in her life; and she remained optimistic about her future.

... making Backstage a 100 million dollar plus assets under management fund at the very least and then at least two to three Xing that over the next few years is the least I want to do ... I have a huge stake in Backstage ... I want it to win, I need it to win, and I think it will.[43]

The lesson is not that Hamilton worked hard and thereby reached some of her goals, though that is certainly true. The takeaway is not that Hamilton is an anomaly (there are other Black women–owned VC firms committed to investing in Black founders),[44] neither is her story an indictment on Black women who find themselves struggling or hurting. And perhaps most important, Hamilton's recent challenges are not proof that the system is unbeatable, her dreams unattainable. The *étude*, rather, is the effectiveness of the Lemonade Lifestyle. It is the ability to create a world of one's own making, notwithstanding harsh realities and circumstances. It means staying in the game and not giving up.

Hamilton lives a Lemonade Lifestyle. She is motivated and driven by purpose and she has an attitude of perseverance. She has learned how to face challenges and to fight for the life she wants to live. Hamilton understands that as she chases after her purpose, she must pursue rest, fun, and joy. Hamilton, like so many Black women who are descendants of African slaves brought to the Americas, can control their lives because they desire to, because they can, and because they know their value. Black women have proven that they embody the American Dream by living the Lemonade Lifestyle.

For at least a century, lemonade has served as a metaphor for Black women, showing them how to triumph over life's difficulties and hardships. It is a tactic that many Black women, like Meta Bell Kearse, Agnéz Deréon, and Hattie White have used to overcome great obstacles. Some may believe that the lemons Black women face are too big to overcome, but I learned at an early age to reject any notion that disavows agency.

For some Black folks, my perspective may be challenging, uninformed, even sacrilegious. Like the scars on my legs, they only see the remnants of damage. They are very good at pointing out the real and problematic legacy of slavery and all the ways it is rooted in the systematic oppression Black folks encounter every day. But just as Jesus showed Thomas the physical scars left by the nails hammered into his hands as a sign that he had risen from the dead, Black women's scars are also a manifestation of victory.

* * *

Weeks after the release of *Lemonade*, the late Black feminist scholar bell hooks wrote a scathing critique of the album and artist, most notably pulling Beyoncé's feminist card, "her construction of feminism cannot be trusted. Her vision of feminism does not call for an end to patriarchal domination."[45] The essay was instantly controversial (how could a Black feminist icon go after a Black pop icon?) with commentaries from Melissa Harris-Perry and Jamilah Lemieux to Roxane Gay.

While most were largely critical of hooks' criticism, there is an incisive moment in her analysis that is worthy of deference and respect:

To truly be free, we must choose beyond simply surviving adversity, we must dare to create lives of sustained optimal well-being and joy. In that world, the making and drinking of lemonade will be a fresh and zestful delight, a real-life mixture of the bitter and the sweet, and not a measure of our capacity to endure pain, but rather a celebration of our moving beyond pain.[46]

In those two sentences, hooks is wisdom personified. The gift of Black women's agency is the choice to live beyond just enduring, just making it through. Instead, hooks challenges Black women not to take stock in how much pain we can endure but to celebrate moving beyond pain. The Lemonade Lifestyle is not just in making it to the other side. It is cultivating wellbeing, joy, and love.

Like lemonade, forging ahead is a bittersweet cocktail. It means examining our relationships, reassessing friendships, coming to new understandings, and making tough decisions about whether the people in our circle are helping us up or have their knee on our necks.

CHAPTER 4

A HOUSE DIVIDED

It was Sunday night, New Year's Day 2017. I sat curled on my couch watching *60 Minutes.*

> *(Organizer) "No more guns!"*
> *(Crowd) "No more guns!"*
> *(Organizer) "Peace in the streets!"*
> *(Crowd) "Peace in the streets!"*[1]

A young boy marched with the activists. No more than nine or ten, he pushed his bike down the dimly lit Chicago streets. Turning slightly, he looked into the camera's lens. Vulnerability and innocence emanated from his eyes.

The image tugged at my heart. I had so many questions. Why was he marching at night? Why did he appear to be alone? Was anyone watching out for him? But the fourteen-minute piece by *60 Minutes* correspondent Bill Whitaker did not focus on the boy, although his fate was tied to the grim realities of the CBS News story.

There was an alarming surge of violence in Chicago—over seven hundred homicides and four thousand shooting victims in 2016, more than Los Angeles and New York combined. In the story, Whitaker revealed data sourced from the Chicago Police Department:

> as killings rose, police activity fell. In August of 2015, cops stopped and questioned 49,257 people. A year later those stops dropped to 8,859, down 80 percent. At the same time arrests were off by a third, from just over 10,000 to 6,900.[2]

According to Whitaker, a dozen rank and file police officers confirmed, off camera, that they had stepped "back from taking proactive action"[3] following public outrage over an officer's shooting death of a Black male teenager.

In 2014, Laquan McDonald, seventeen, was fatally shot by a white policeman. The dash cam footage of the deadly encounter was released via court order a year later and it contradicted the officer's account. The video showed McDonald being shot sixteen times—many of the bullets striking him after he had walked away, even as he laid crumbled on the ground. The unjust killing fueled protests, heightened racial tensions between the city and residents, and increased public scrutiny of the Chicago Police Department.

The *60 Minutes* piece reported that "within six weeks of the shooting scandal, investigative stops fell by nearly 35,000. That's when the violence began to surge."[4] While CBS was careful to acknowledge the impact that "gangs, guns and drugs"[5] may have had on the increase of gun violence and the sharp rise in murders, their supposition was impossible to miss: CPD inaction was likely the cause.

I vaguely heard the signature sound of the ticking clock. *60 Minutes* had moved on to its next story. But I was no longer paying attention. My mind was focused inward. I raged against the images, the statistics. I railed against white supremacy, poverty, and the criminal justice system, oppression ensnaring so many Black men and boys.

As I mulled over the story that January evening, I did not realize until much later that it had erased Black women. But then, why would I notice? The reporting and imagery centered on footage of Black men in handcuffs, Black men resisting arrest, a Black man shot to death by another Black man, and the dash cam video killing of McDonald. On-camera interviews followed the same pattern; Whitaker spoke to Black male police officers and to a few white men who served as law enforcement experts. During the entire report, only one Black woman spoke—useful to the national conversation as a mourner only. Her life—her narrative—eclipsed by the tragic death of her son.

Based on the reporting, a *60 Minutes'* viewer could surmise that in Chicago in 2016, bullets did not pierce the bodies of Black women and girls. But that would be an inaccurate assumption. In May of that year, Yvonne Nelson,[6] forty-nine, was shot outside of a Starbucks after purchasing a cup of tea. Nykea Aldridge,[7] mother of four, was shot and killed that August while pushing her baby in a stroller on Chicago's South Side. And Sakinah Reed,[8] seventeen, was shot to death in January 2016 while standing outside. These are just a few examples of Chicagoan Black women and teen girls killed by gun violence that year.

And there were police shooting deaths of Black women in Chicago, stories that should have been known to CBS: Rekia Boyd,[9] twenty-two, shot and killed by an off-duty officer in 2012 and a fifty-five-year-old grandmother, Bettie Jones,[10] who was shot by CPD in 2015. And yet, the all-male reporting team reduced Black women to a sideshow in a drama focused on rescuing, remediating, and restoring the lives of Black men and boys.

Intentionally or unintentionally, Whitaker, a Black man, reinforced patriarchy within the Black community. Historically, Black culture has prioritized Black men. This manifests in the prioritization of Black men's pain over the pain of Black women, of Black men's rights over the rights of Black women, and the expectation that Black women are obligated to support Black men, even to their own detriment. The lives of Black men have simply mattered more.

In 1986, Dr. Gerda Lerner, a second-wave feminist and pioneer of the study of women's history, published the *Creation of Patriarchy*.

In an interview for the *New York Times* that year, Lerner described patriarchy as a four-thousand-year-old system that has gone through several iterations.[11] From one based on a form of social organization in which the father or eldest male headed a family or tribe to today where patriarchy is an institutionalized pattern of male dominance, Lerner explained:

> I show that [patriarchy] was indeed a human invention . . .
> it was created by men and women at a certain given point in
> the historical development of the human race. It was probably appropriate as a solution for the problems of that time,
> which was the Bronze Age, but it's no longer appropriate. [12]

Patriarchy is an entrenched system, and it is global. But it is also harmful and without purpose in the twenty-first century. And, as Lerner pointed out, patriarchy is a "cultur[al] invention, not a natural or inevitable phenomenon."[13] In other words, patriarchy, a social construct birthed by human design, can be ended by human intervention.

* * *

The horrific murders of Emmett Till, Trayvon Martin, and George Floyd were the catalysts for national and global movements to a degree that the murders of Black women and girls—like Rekia Boyd, Breonna Taylor, or the four girls killed in the 1963 Birmingham church bombing—never seem to inspire.

Till's murder in 1955 was the tipping point for the mid-twentieth-century social movements for racial justice. According to the Martin Luther King, Jr., Research and Education Institute at Stanford University, "Just three months after Till's body was pulled from the Tallahatchie River, the Montgomery bus boycott began,"[14] launching the Civil Rights Movement.

The murder of Martin, a Florida teen, in 2012 was the impetus for the Black Lives Matter Movement (BLM). Three Black women—Alicia Garza, Patrisse Khan-Cullors, and Ayọ Tometi (formerly known as Opal Tometi)—founded the movement. In a filmed interview for *Time* magazine, Garza shared how BLM began:

> What prompted Black Lives Matter was really around the murder of Trayvon Martin . . . I wrote a Facebook post: "black people. I love you. I love us. Our lives matter. black lives matter." Patrisse put a hashtag in front of it . . . And Opal said, this is brilliant, and I think we should build something that connects people online and get people to do stuff together offline.[15]

For nine minutes and twenty-nine seconds, former Minneapolis Police officer Derek Chauvin knelt on George Floyd's neck. On May 25, 2020, a young Black woman, Darnella Frazier, videotaped on her phone the shocking footage of the white cop killing

Floyd, who was unarmed. Video of Floyd calling out for his late mother, and the callousness of Chauvin's barbarity rekindled the Black Lives Matter movement.

The *New York Times* reported on the months-long historic protests that followed Floyd's murder, "Four recent polls suggest that about fifteen million to twenty-six million people in the United States have participated in demonstrations over the death of George Floyd and others in recent weeks. These figures would make the recent protests the largest movement in the country's history."[16] It is not a coincidence that a Black man's death ignited protests around the world.

Without question, the murders of Black men like Eric Garner, Mike Brown, Tamir Rice, Oscar Grant, Ahmaud Arbery, and Daunte Wright have dominated the Black Lives Matter movement. The irony isn't lost on BLM co-founder Khan-Cullors in a *Washington Post* interview: "stories of police encounters with [B]lack Americans have largely centered on men. 'We don't talk about what experience criminalization has on our bodies . . . We just become the vehicle to tell black men's stories.'"[17] Patriarchy, within and outside the Black community, best explains the erasure of Black women.

Nearly seventy years span the murders of Till, Martin, and Floyd and the movements that spawned from their tragic deaths, but the visceral, galvanizing reaction to the pain of Black men and boys hasn't changed. Patriarchy and the value placed on the male sex, even those who are Black and Brown, continue to trigger an emotional response in the collective psyche.

Following the police killing of Michael Brown in 2014, the *Washington Post* started compiling every fatal shooting by an on-duty police officer in the United States. The data and what it reveals is important in many ways, but I am going to highlight just three areas of interest to me. First, Blacks are killed by the police at more than twice the rate of whites. Second, the majority of people shot and killed by police are male (more than 95 percent). And third, more than half the victims are between the ages of twenty and forty.[18]

The data is clear; young Black men are more likely to be victims of police shooting deaths. The issue that I raise isn't simply about the attention Black men and boys receive. Facts prove that the attention is warranted, right, and necessary for change to ensue. My issue is with a stark reality—police murders of Black women rarely, if ever, touch a similar societal nerve.

* * *

Patriarchy is essential to understanding the existent power dynamics betwixt Black women and men, and how it manifests in social movements and in the Black Church.

For decades, Black feminists have been sounding an alarm: the Black community is not exempt from patriarchy. Despite the warnings and work of notable Black feminists—Barbara Smith, Beverly Smith, bell hooks, Audre Lorde, Alice Walker, June Jordan, Brittney Cooper, Roxane Gay, and Feminista Jones, to name a few—within Black culture it remains challenging to acknowledge or confront patriarchy.

In 1977, a collective of Black feminists famously released a paper called the *Combahee River Collective Statement*. It is a manifesto that addresses four key topics, including the difficulties encountered in recruiting Black women to join their movement:

Feminism is, nevertheless, very threatening to the majority of Black people because it calls into question some of the most basic assumptions about our existence, i.e., that

sex should be a determinant of power relationships. Many
Black women have a good understanding of both sexism
and racism, but because of the everyday constrictions of
their lives, cannot risk struggling against them both. The
reaction of Black men to feminism has been notoriously
negative . . . accusations that Black feminism divides the
Black struggle are powerful deterrents to the growth of an
autonomous Black women's movement.[19]

The concerns outlined by the Combahee River Collective over
forty years ago remain central to Black women's reticence in
challenging patriarchy and embracing the empowerment of
feminist ideals. The notion that Black feminism means anti–
Black men, thereby delaying freedom for all Black people, continues to be an impediment for many Black women.

The dichotomy between Black women's awareness of sexism
within the Black community and the will to challenge patriarchy
in pursuit of Black women's rights emerges in the exclusive Marist
Poll survey conducted for this book. When we asked how much
of a problem sex discrimination is against Black women in the
Black community, 95 percent of Black women say it is a problem
to some degree, whereas just 4 percent say it's not a problem. This
viewpoint is consistent, regardless of the respondent's age, income,
education, or how urban or rural they describe where they live.

But when we asked Black women if they think it is more
important for Black women to fight for the rights of all Black people, to fight for the rights of all Black women, or if both are equally
important, more than six in ten Black women (61 percent) say it
is equally important for Black women to fight for the rights of all
Black people and all Black women.

Although there is consensus that fighting for the rights of
all Black women and all Black people are equally important,

interestingly, 27 percent of Gen Z/Millennials are more likely than Gen Xers (8 percent) and Baby Boomers (2 percent) to say that it is more important for Black women to fight for the rights of all Black women. When the conflicting answers are juxtaposed, the paradox is clear. While Black women are cognizant of the negative impact of sexism in their community and how it shows up in private and public spaces, they understand Black men and their complex, often fragile masculinity. For a Black woman to operate in full badassery is threatening.

I have an aunt who is the epitome of cool. Smart, witty, charming, confident, and wise with a strong sense of self, she is dope*ness*. Twenty years ago, she gave me this advice. "If you're ever out to eat with your man and he's struggling financially and doesn't have any money, slip him some money under the table so he can pay the bill." That way, she told me, he won't look or feel bad as a man.

I followed this advice once or twice over the years, and I hadn't given it much thought until recently. My aunt's advice is incongruent to dope*ness*. It is making oneself small so someone else feels big. How does my greatness (or in this case, the fact that I have money) diminish a Black man or hurt him? My aunt's dating advice is indicative of the Black woman's conflict with patriarchy. My aunt is very self-assured and isn't shy about communicating her wants or needs, but that particular lesson reinforced norms that Black women are required to support patriarchy, even though we're well aware that sexism runs unchecked in the Black community.

The late cultural critic bell hooks addressed patriarchy in an interview in 2016,

There has been an inordinate focus on black masculinity and the assumption that the way to liberate black men is through patriarchy ... that constant focus on black masculinity tends to obfuscate and take away meaningful attention from black females. The narrative of liberation in the US almost always ends up in terms of black people valorizing patriarchy.[20]

The correlation between Black liberation and patriarchy is supported by a faulty, yet enduring premise: if Black men win, Black women do too.

The totality of Black women's lived experiences is best understood via an intersectional prism—a term credited to Kimberlé Crenshaw, though a decade earlier the women of the Combahee River Collective described a similar dynamic they called "interlocking." Crenshaw, a leading scholar and writer on civil rights and Black feminist legal theory, described intersectionality for the first time in an academic paper published in the University of Chicago's Legal Forum in 1989:

Black women can experience discrimination in ways that are both similar to and different from those experienced by white women and Black men. Black women sometimes experience discrimination in ways similar to white women's experiences; sometimes they share very similar experiences with Black men. Yet often they experience double discrimination—the combined effects of practices which discriminate on the basis of race, and on the basis of sex.[21]

This theory is essential in understanding the intersecting systems of oppression Black women confront on a daily basis. And Crenshaw argued that patriarchy was "another source of domination to which Black women are vulnerable."[22]

* * *

Perhaps the first time the rights of Black men took precedence over the rights of Black women was at the brink of emancipation. It was the twilight of the Civil War, and another battle, this one of the heart and mind, was brewing. Abolitionist and formerly enslaved Frederick Douglass was at the forefront of an ideological struggle.

Speaking before the Massachusetts Anti-Slavery Society in 1865, Douglass was clear on who and what he was fighting for: "I am for the immediate, unconditional, and universal enfranchisement of the black man, in every State in the Union."[23] There were those who argued slavery should be abolished first and then the rights of suffrage would be "extended to the negro." Douglass disagreed with this approach. He favored pushing for suffrage while the treatment of Black folks was at the forefront of the nation's consciousness.

Douglass understood that without the right to vote, "negro men" would be deprived of their full rights, "We want it because it is our right, first of all. No class of men can, without insulting their own nature, be content with any deprivation of their rights."[24]

Contrary to his impassioned plea, Douglass had once been an ardent supporter of universal suffrage. Nearly two decades earlier, he had labored alongside women's rights pioneers Susan B. Anthony and Elizabeth Cady Stanton. In 1848, he attended the first women's rights convention in Seneca Falls, New York. But when it appeared that Congress would confer the right to vote on "Black men but not women of any race," Douglass threw his support behind the Fifteenth Amendment.

In *When and Where I Enter*, historian Paula Giddings notes that Black women had to decide whether or not to support the

Fifteenth Amendment. Some abolitionists like "Sojourner Truth took the position of not supporting the amendment. She was fearful that putting more power in to the hands of [Black] men would add to the oppression of Black women."[25] But most Black women, like abolitionist and poet Frances Ellen Harper, supported Douglass and Black male suffrage:

> The support of the Fifteenth Amendment by Black women did not mean that they had less interest in their suffrage, economic independence, education, or any other issue that pertained to them. And their support certainly didn't mean a collective willingness to be oppressed by men, Black or white. But Harper and others understood that the rights of Black men had to be secured before Black women could assert theirs.[26]

Five years after the Civil War, Black men gained the right to vote when the Fifteenth Amendment was ratified in 1870. White women suffragists, frustrated and angry that Black men could vote before them, worked with renewed vigor. They secured the right to vote in 1920, a full fifty years later.

However, Black women were not afforded unfettered access to the ballot box until the passage of the Voting Rights Act of 1965. The battle for suffrage cemented the idea that race took precedence over gender—a mindset that inherently benefited Black men. For Black women, to choose one identity over the other guaranteed intersectional oppression.

* * *

Roughly two thousand gathered in Memphis at Mason Temple Church of God in Christ on April 3, 1968. At the time, Mason

Temple was the largest church building in the United States owned by a Black Christian denomination. Undeterred by inclement weather, the crowd hung onto the preacher's every word.

Some historians have cited "I've Been to the Mountaintop" as one of Dr. Martin Luther King Jr.'s best sermons. In part, because it was his last. Less than twenty-four hours later, King would be killed. Shot by a single assassin's bullet.

His death imminent, the Civil Rights leader stood behind the pulpit, his voice rising at the apogee—his words prescient:

> . . . and [God has] allowed me to go up to the mountain. And I've looked over, and I've seen the Promised Land. I may not get there with you. But I want you to know tonight, that we, as a people, will get to the Promised Land. And so, I'm happy tonight; I'm not worried about anything; I'm not fearing any man. Mine eyes have seen the glory of the coming of the Lord.[27]

As a child, I was taught to hope in and watch for King's Promised Land, a Black utopia, to come to fruition. A place where melanin is no longer analogous to inferiority. But as an adult, I had become more discerning.

King began the sermon by thanking and acknowledging close friend and civil rights activist Ralph Abernathy. He lauded others, pastors he described as "noble men . . . in this struggle,"[28] James Lawson, Ralph Jackson, Billy Kyles, and Jesse Jackson. But like the *60 Minutes* report, Black women's lived experiences and contributions were overlooked, erased, and ignored.

King failed to thank one Black woman that night. Not Ella Baker and Septima Poinsette Clark, women who worked directly with King at the Southern Christian Leadership Conference

(SCLC). Even Coretta Scott King, his wife of fifteen years, was deemed unworthy of *réclame*. But just as significant is the story King choose to share with the Memphis crowd:

> Several years ago, I was in New York City autographing the first book that I had written. And while sitting there autographing books, a demented Black woman came up. The only question I heard from her was, "Are you Martin Luther King?" And I was looking down writing and I said, "Yes" . . . Before I knew it, I had been stabbed by this demented woman.[29]

The incident occurred on September 20, 1958. King, then twenty-nine, was signing autographs for his first book, *Stride Toward Freedom: The Montgomery Story*. The *New York Times* provided details of the attack and attacker:

> [Izola Ware Curry] entered the store armed with a loaded .25-caliber automatic pistol and the letter opener. The pistol was secreted in her bra, the letter opener in her handbag. She pushed her way through the crowd to the table where Dr. King sat. "Are you Martin Luther King?" she asked. "Yes," he replied, not looking up from the book he was signing. She reached into her handbag . . . He was taken to Harlem Hospital, where surgeons opened his chest and ever so gently withdrew the blade. Ms. Curry was apprehended in the store. "I've been after him for six years," she cried. "I'm glad I done it."[30]

A photo of the attack ran the next day in the *New York Daily News*, King slouched in a chair surrounded by anxious onlookers—a seven-inch ivory-handled letter opener protruding from his chest.

It was a harrowing story. In hindsight, recounting a near-death experience seems eerily apropos. But it strikes me that the only time King mentions a Black woman in his speech, it was in reference to one who had hurt him, a Black woman he repeatedly called "demented." It is improbable he simply forgot to recognize Black women. King knew Black women had also suffered the sting of the fire hose, the blows from the police baton, and the taunts of hate-spewing racists. He witnessed and benefited from their organizing, planning, and strategizing acumen. Given the adherence to patriarchal norms within the Black Church, I posit that King did not think it was necessary to publicly thank and praise Black women's contributions to the freedom struggle. His erasure, like the slavery economy that forced African descendant women to be bred like cattle, reduced Black women to nameless, faceless laborers.

King's words—spoken or written—serve as a time capsule and a signifier for whom and what was important to him and thereby the movement. More than half a century after his speech, the full body of Black women's contributions and leadership within the Civil Rights Movement remains largely unknown and unacknowledged by the general public. This is how history gets written. It is how Black women are pushed to the margins of historical narratives.

This is not a vanity play. For Black women, the stories of their foremothers help to motivate, encourage, and keep them moving onward. It is how, as discussed in chapter one, Black women saw a high rate of growth in real median wages, completion of four years or more of college, and in the number of professional roles. History is a Black women's birthright and inspiration.

The *Combahee River Collective Statement* provides context for King's oversight as part of a larger dynamic within Black social movements:

[Black men are threatened] that Black feminists might organize around our own needs. They realize that they might not only lose valuable and hardworking allies in their struggles but that they might also be forced to change their habitually sexist ways of interacting with and oppressing Black women.[31]

Upon closer inspection, this is not the first nor only time King had undermined Black women, regulating them to the back of the proverbial bus.

In every black and white photo that I could find of Septima Poinsette Clark, her bearing rarely diverged: head held high, shoulders straight, eyes framed by glasses. Maybe her disposition took root as a child of the Jim Crow South, progeny of a slave. Perhaps the pain of losing her infant daughter and then a husband to kidney failure broke her heart. Or maybe being a Black woman in the United States dedicated to freedom work necessitated a no-nonsense comportment.

Then I found another photo. Clark is seated in a lawn chair, looking directly into the camera. Salt and pepper hair brushed back. Mouth slightly open. It's one of the rare times Clark is pictured without her distinctive glasses. Her eyes give me pause. I imagine they reflect a figurative rod of steel fixed along the length of her spine, a source of inner determination and conviction. Suddenly, the photos make sense. Clark chooses to be sober. The stakes too high; her life's work too important.

By the time King rose to national prominence in the mid-1950s, Clark had been a public-school teacher for forty years and an active member of the National Association for the Advancement of Colored People (NAACP). In 1945, Clark worked with Thurgood Marshall and the NAACP on a class-action lawsuit that sought parity between Black and white teachers' pay in Columbia, South Carolina. The NAACP won that case and Clark's salary tripled. Clark described the victory in her autobiography, *Echo in My Soul*, "I would call it my first effort in a social action challenging the status quo . . . I felt that in reality I was working for the accomplishment of something that ultimately would be good for everyone."[32]

More than a decade later, South Carolina's state legislature passed a law prohibiting public employees from participating in the NAACP. Clark refused to renounce her membership and was subsequently fired. Unemployment pushed the teacher, now budding activist, further into social action. Clark became the director of workshops at the Highlander Folk School in Tennessee, a training ground for Black folks and other people working toward a more just society.

Clark's experience at the Highlander Folk School led to the development of a curriculum she called Citizenship Schools. Pairing education and activism, the program taught "Blacks how to read and write their names so they could pass literacy tests and be eligible to vote. Students also learned life skills . . . and democratic principles, including the United States Constitution, the way government works and how to vote in elections."[33]

The success of the Citizenship Schools caught the attention of King and the Southern Christian Leadership Conference (SCLC). In 1961, Clark migrated Citizenship Schools to SCLC, becoming the director of education and teaching.

Prior to joining the prominent civil rights organization, Clark asked fellow organizer Ella Baker what it was like for women to work at SCLC. One of its original architects, Baker had recently left to increase the participation of college students in the movement. Her efforts culminated with the formation of the Student Nonviolent Coordinating Committee

(SNCC)—a civil rights organization that birthed the Black Power movement.

Clark shared details of her conversations with Baker in a 1976 interview conducted by the University of North Carolina at Chapel Hill. Retired by this time and well into her seventies, Clark told the interviewer that SCLC "didn't respect women too much,"[34] and they were not encouraged to speak during executive meetings, "if we had anything to say, maybe we could get to say it at the end of the session, but we never were able to put ourselves on the agenda to speak to the group."[35] Clark recounted one particularly demeaning experience:

> **Interviewer:** And you tried to get on the agenda of the executive committee to talk about this problem and...
> **Clark:** Didn't get any support. No. I couldn't get it done.
> **Interviewer:** How did they keep you from being on the agenda?
> **Clark:** Just didn't put it on. I wrote the letter, and then no mention was made. Dr. King made mention one time of a letter that I sent to him, and he was really laughing about it, and nobody answered. And nobody would say anything.[36]

In Clark's letter to King, she suggested that other activists besides King get an opportunity to lead marches. Instead of giving Clark—a woman thirty years his senior, a woman who had worked for decades as an activist before he was born, a woman whose work enabled thousands of Black people to vote—an opportunity to speak, King laughed at her in front of their colleagues during an executive meeting.

The sexism Clark and Baker experienced at SCLC was endemic to the Civil Rights Movement. In their book, *A Black Women's History of the United States,* historians Daina Ramey Berry and Kali Nicole Gross wrote about the challenges other female activists encountered:

> Even when they obtained leadership positions, as Gwendolyn Zohara [*sic*] Simmons, a member of SNCC who worked on the Mississippi Freedom Summer Project, explained, she "often had to struggle around issues related to a woman being a project director. We had to fight for the resources, you know. We had to fight to get a good car because the guys would get first dibs on everything, and that wasn't fair . . . It was a struggle to be taken seriously by the leadership, as well as by your male colleagues . . . One of the things that we often don't talk about, but there was sexual harassment that often happened toward the women."[37]

Once again, patriarchy and sexism provide the context for the intersectional subjugation Black women experienced as they continued to fight alongside Black men throughout the Civil Rights and Black liberation social movements.

* * *

On January 26, 2020, NBA superstar Kobe Bryant, his thirteen-year-old daughter Gianna, and seven others were killed in a helicopter crash in Calabasas, California. The death of the basketball legend and his young daughter was a huge story, momentarily eclipsing the impeachment of President Donald

Trump in the House of Representatives and the subsequent Senate trial.

Days later, *CBS This Morning* anchor Gayle King interviewed Lisa Leslie, a former WNBA player and long-time friend of Bryant. King asked, "It's been said that his legacy is complicated because of a sexual assault charge which was dismissed in 2003, 2004. Is it complicated for you, as a woman, as a WNBA player?"[38]

In 2003, Bryant had been charged with one count of felony assault for allegedly raping a nineteen-year-old woman. Prosecutors later dropped the case because the accuser decided not to testify. Two years later, a civil suit brought by the accuser was settled out of court.

Reaction to King's question was swift and brutal—emphasizing the idea that Black women are expected to support Black men at all costs. Rapper Snoop Dogg took to Instagram, posting a profanity-laced video that has since been deleted:

> Gayle King, you're out of pocket for that shit . . . Way out of pocket. What do you gain from that? We expect more from you Gayle . . . Why are you all attacking us? We're your people. You don't come after Harvey Weinstein asking those dumbass questions. I'm sick of y'all. Funky doghead bitch. How dare you try to torch my homeboy's reputation? Punk motherfucker. Respect the family and back off, bitch, before we come get you.[39]

Snoop Dogg's post was followed by similar comments from rapper and actor 50 Cent. LeBron James, a close friend of Bryant and former Team USA teammate, tweeted in part, "We are our own worse [*sic*] enemies!"[40]

Although Snoop Dogg later apologized "for being disrespectful"[41] following a conversation with his mother, the fallout was painful for King. A few months later in an interview with her best friend, Oprah Winfrey, King had some perspective, "What got to me was the vitriol and the vulgarity that was just unleashed at me in ways that I could not even understand where that was coming from . . . it's just not fair or okay to be as vulgar and as hateful as what I experienced."[42] Publicly, King expressed a lack of understanding, but privately I wouldn't be surprised if she knew exactly what was going on: patriarchy, sexism, and misogyny were at work.

King had violated an unspoken commandment in the Black community: *Thou shalt not disparage Black men*. And she had defied a golden rule: *Black women uplift Black men, always and especially in public*. It is why Snoop Dogg incredulously asked, "Why are you all attacking us?" The "you all" being Black women, and "us" being Black men. And it also explains why he mentioned the disgraced film director and convicted sex offender Harvey Weinstein. The supposition: a Black woman can disrespect a white man, but a Black man?

Snoop Dogg perceives King's question as an assault on all Black men, rather than a question about an individual. Similarly, LeBron James's admonishment, "We are our own worse [sic] enemies!," demonstrates a belief that King's question about one man harms all Black people.

As an award-winning, seasoned, celebrated journalist, King has earned the right to ask whatever question she deems appropriate. I grew up watching King in the 1980s and 1990s when she was a news anchor at the CBS affiliate WFSB in Hartford, Connecticut. My grandmother, mother, aunts, and everyone I knew respected and looked up to her as one of the only Black women anchoring the local news in our area. I knew King as a journalist well before the world knew her as Oprah's best friend. And the idea that anyone would tell Gayle King how to do her job is utterly ridiculous.

But to Black men who think like Snoop Dogg, Lebron James, and 50 Cent, King's accomplishments and position as an elder within the Black community were inconsequential. King's rights were secondary to protecting and uplifting a Black man, and by proxy all Black people.

The more successful the Black man, the higher his status is within the Black community. Cultural norms seek to protect Black men against anyone or anything that would threaten that success—hence the rabid reaction to King's question.

This dynamic is further substantiated by the Black community's reluctance to accept the accusations lobbied against comedian and actor Bill Cosby. Although Cosby's 2018 convictions on charges of drugging and sexually assaulting a Temple University employee were vacated in 2021, there are still dozens of women who allege that he drugged and assaulted them. And even Cosby, when he was still in prison, thought he had a right to criticize King in a tweet directed to @SnoopDogg and his millions of followers, "@SnoopDogg . . . It's so sad and disappointing that successful Black women are being used to tarnish the image and legacy of successful Black Men, even in death."[43]

The Black golden rule also gives context for why it took two decades before a majority of Black people, according to a 2015 *Washington Post*-ABC News poll, believed O. J. Simpson likely killed Nicole Brown Simpson and Ron Goldman.[44]

Since 1996, the Violence Policy Center (VPC) has released data on the number of women murdered by males in the United States. In 2019, the most recent year for which information is available, Black women (2.34 per 100,000) were murdered by males at a rate more than twice as high as white women and girls (0.99 per 100,000).[45] Where the relationship could be determined, 91 percent of Black women and girls killed by males in single-victim/

single-offender incidents knew their killers. Of Black victims who knew their offenders, 60 percent were wives, common-law wives, ex-wives, or girlfriends of the offenders.[46] Nearly all (93 percent) of the homicides of Black females were intra-racial, which means 93 percent of the perpetuators were Black males.[47]

Add to this disturbing picture that Black women have one of the highest rates of both domestic violence and sexual abuse victimization than any other ethnic/racial group. The National Intimate Partner and Sexual Violence Survey found that 45 percent of Black women experienced contact sexual violence, physical violence, and/or stalking by an intimate partner in their lifetime, and 21 percent of Black women report being raped during their lifetime.[48]

The numbers are staggering, but they reflect a long-standing trend. For decades, government studies have shown that Black women consistently suffer violence at the hands of their intimate partners, men who tend to be Black. In an interview about high rates of Black women and girls murdered in the United States, Black feminist legal scholar Kimberlé Crenshaw had this to say, "there's never been a moment in our society where there's been a reckoning with the particular kinds of violence that's meted out against Black women."[49] I would take it one step further: there hasn't been a reckoning in the Black community either. The prioritization of Black men within the Black community is the complicity of silence.

The system of patriarchy also insists on the dominance of men within the Black Church, regardless of the denomination. In chapter two, I addressed the centrality of faith for many Black women. When Black men are compared to Black women, a Pew Research Center analysis found that Black men are less religious than Black women: 69 percent of Black men say religion is very important to them, compared with 80 percent of Black women.[50] The same survey found that "Black men (70 percent) are less likely than Black women (83 percent) to be categorized as highly religious."[51] On any Sunday morning, visit any predominately Black church in the United States and the data confirms what Black folks already know: the pews are filled largely with Black women and the pulpits are mostly dominated by Black men. While there are more women in leadership positions in Black churches than ever before, women are still more likely to toil behind the scenes, doing the grunt work necessary to ensure the business of the church gets done.

Within the confines of the Black Church, Black men have historically benefited from the same systems of oppression that have disempowered them for centuries. The prevalence of patriarchy in the pulpits and pews bestows power and authority. Black men have garnered respect by emulating patriarchy and capitalism, holding power over the souls, bodies, and pocketbooks of Black women.

In chapter one, I introduced Alisha Gordon, a forty-year-old Black woman who graduated from seminary in 2015. Gordon grew up in Georgia steeped in the traditions of the Black Church. Her father was a deacon and trustee at a southern missionary Baptist church, and she spent her childhood at church several days a week:

Women don't preach, wear pants or lipstick. Patriarchy and misogyny are interwoven in the church . . . You think about being a twelve-year-old girl, sitting in somebody's church, you got this man in the pulpit, by proximity already over you by design of the building, tell you that your body is unholy. That your knee showing is bringing a man to fall. All of that is tied to patriarchal norms.[52]

Speaking from first-hand experience, Gordon believes that patriarchy in the pulpit teaches Black girls to be ashamed of their bodies, while teaching Black boys they don't have to take responsibility for their actions.

In 2018, theologian Candice Marie Benbow wrote an article for a digital lifestyle website titled, "I'm A Single Christian Woman And I Like Sex." The story lit up Black Twitter, went viral, and predictably became controversial. Raised in a Black Missionary Baptist Church, Benbow had participated in the normative religious mores of abstinence. But as a practitioner of womanist theology that challenged the patriarchal status quo, Benbow rearticulated sexuality for Christian Black women:

> I believe Jesus when he said that he came to give us abundant life. Denying myself real pleasure and deep joy contradicts that. Believing that I am not supposed to experience the intimacy God designed my body for until I'm married devalues creation and is just ridiculous. What if I never get married? Should I not still experience physical pleasure and joy? There is something unholy about a God who would require that I maneuver through this anti-Black, anti-woman world without a soft place to land.[53]

In her book, *Red Lip Theology: For Church Girls Who've Considered Tithing to the Beauty Supply Store When Sunday Morning Isn't Enough*, Benbow's rejection of chastity is rooted in a commitment to "recognize and denounce the patriarchal and sexist foundations of religious and intuitional church spaces."[54]

The main driver of gender inequality in the Black Church is a theological framework that promulgates the inferiority, weakness, and submissiveness of women. It is a theology founded on the idea that God made women unequal to men and women are forever punished by Eve's original sin of taking the first bite of the apple offered by Satan. Like Benbow, a growing, though small, number of Black women are using Biblical evidence to support gender equality.

In 2017, Taffi Dollar, who serves as the founder and senior pastor of World Changers Church International along with her husband, televangelist Creflo Dollar, published *Gender Roles.* Dollar admits to having "struggled for thirty years with [the idea of] submissiveness. I just couldn't believe that, based on my gender, I was to forever yield to someone else based solely on his gender."[55]

In 2016, Taffi Dollar attended a conference in South Africa hosted by Christians for Biblical Equality. She writes of a transformation, a reframing informed by scholars steeped in Bible-based gender equality, "I learned to look closer at biblical references that had been misinterpreted and misappropriated to perpetuate a hierarchy—a world-wide system of patriarchy, with women at the bottom of the totem pole."[56] In the book, Dollar dissects scriptures that are well-known to church folk, making a deliberate, impassioned case for gender equality.

Dollar is now on a mission to evangelize people in the pews: "When we understand that God created both men and women in his own image, we can begin to understand, respect, embrace, and appreciate one another's God-given gifts. Operating in our gifts without gender limitations can empower women and men."[57]

I may not agree with all of Dollar's analysis and ideas, but a Bible-based theology debunking patriarchy is a step in the right direction.

*　*　*

Like the bonds shared by Black women, Black men and women are also connected by enslavement and oppression, as well as in the hope inspired by collective resistance and commitment to liberation. That bond, forged on slave ships and in cotton and tobacco fields, is why patriarchy in the Black community is so painful and often feels like betrayal. For nearly two centuries, Black women have faithfully partnered with Black men to achieve freedom—not for a certain kind of Black person, but for all Black people.

Patriarchy was built for and to benefit white men. And for Black men, it is self-defeating. Not only is it wrong for Black men to utilize patriarchy, but it is substantially egregious when the battle for liberation has not been fully won. Black folks in the United States have made great strides; but a house divided cannot stand. I posit that Black women will never fully stand with Black men or completely trust them until patriarchy is utterly and completely obliterated.

My Black sisters. We walk a tightrope, balancing the rights and needs of Black men against our own. We prioritize our sons, brothers, and fathers, motivated by a love to insulate them from systems of oppression. We've soothed egos and helped Black men believe in themselves. We've prodded, pushed, and needled Black men to enable them to reach their highest potential. And to do this, some of us dim our light, sideline our dreams, and make ourselves smaller. The truth is, we love and support our Black men, but it should never endanger our wellbeing or hinder our potential.

My Black brothers. Black men face enormous obstacles and barriers to living whole, healthy, and fulfilling lives. But so do Black women. Take heed of the results of the Marist Poll, that found 95 percent of Black women said that some form of sex discrimination exists in the Black community. It is abhorrent to lean on patriarchy when Black women have consistently supported Black men. And though I know many good, honest, caring, supportive Black men (like my father and other family members), too many vent their anger, frustrations, and fists on Black women when the enemy, in the words of bell hooks, is the imperialist, white-supremacist, capitalist patriarchy.

Why don't we, Black women, Black men, work together from a mutual place of equality, of respect, and of love to dismantle the systems that seek to destroy us? If we do, not only will we heal our communities, but we'll create a better, brighter future for our children.

CHAPTER 5
UNBRIDGED

Bridges symbolize connection. By design and purpose, they are built over obstacles that separate—water, valleys, roads. But amid a lingering global pandemic, in an age of stark political and cultural divisions, the notion of connection feels at once alien and nostalgic. Bridges remind us of our shared fragmentations, fault lines threading society's underbelly. Borders uncrossed. Barriers unbroken. Boundaries redrawn.

The Amazon River divides—its waters nearly split an entire continent into two parts. The ancient river flows west to east in northern South America. A journey that begins high in the Andes Mountains and meanders through the majestic, lush Amazon Rainforest before it empties into the Atlantic Ocean. Second only to the Nile River in length, 20 percent of the world's fresh-water supply to oceans comes from the Amazon River. Home to more than two thousand species of fish and hundreds of amphibians, the Amazon region is an essential life source for an estimated thirty million people living across eight countries.

The Amazon River is one of Earth's great natural wonders. Still one distinction remains largely unknown: it is the longest river in the world not crossed by a single bridge.

The Amazon River is more than four thousand miles long, and up to thirty miles wide during the rainy season, but that is not the reason it remains unbridged. While it would be expensive and complicated, most civil engineers believe it is technically possible. The Amazon River is bridgeless because the cost of building one exceeds perceived benefits.

Black women and white women are unbridged. And like the continent of South America, they are nearly torn asunder. Relationships divided, not by a powerful river, but by a powerful truth: many Black women do not trust white women.

Emerson University professor Kim McLarin explores distrust between Black and white women in her book, *Womanish: A Grown Black Woman Speaks on Love and Life*:

> Generally speaking . . . I do not trust [white women]. Generally speaking, most Black women don't. That's a big statement . . . This distrust—or, more precisely, this absence of trust—seems to hold true whether or not the Black woman has lived and worked mostly in predominately white environments, whether or not she actually has any white friends, or whether or not she feels this absence as a loss. Most [Black] women [express] a kind of matter-of-fact awareness of the situation.[1]

Trust matters, particularly for interpersonal relationships and group dynamics. Rigorously debated since the time of ancient Greek philosophers, researchers across the social and biological sciences have contributed to the collective understanding of trust.

In a paper published by a peer-reviewed journal, New York University Abu Dhabi professor and sociologist Blaine G. Robbins argued for the adoption of "a single trust concept built around four essential properties: actor A's beliefs, actor B's trustworthiness, the matter [Y] at hand, and unknown outcomes."[2]

Robbins's theory starts with the belief (or disbelief) held by actor A that actor B "will act trustworthily toward actor A with respect to some matter Y."[3] Applying Robbins's single trust theory—where "actor A" represents Black women and "actor B" white women—Black women are not confident white women will behave in a consistently trustworthy manner. It doesn't mean white women are never reliable, but there is a general perception that if the stakes are too high, if it's a "you or me" scenario, trust is more likely to be breached.

In the exclusive survey I conducted in partnership with the Marist Poll in 2021, we asked Black women if they trust white women a great deal, a good amount, not very much, or not at all. While 57 percent of Black women say they trust white women, 43 percent of Black women say they do not trust them very much or at all. In other words, more than four in ten Black women do not trust white women.

For comparison, we also asked Black women if they trust Latina or Asian women. Most Black women trust women of ethnic groups, 70 percent, and 61 percent respectively. And as one might expect, in-group trust is high. When Black women were asked about their level of trust for other Black women, 83 percent of Black women trust other Black women. And nearly 40 percent of Black women say that they trust other Black women a great deal. These findings suggest that Black women have a deep ambivalence toward the trustworthiness of white women, and many are not convinced that white women can or should be trusted.

I asked Alisha Gordon—the Georgia-born single mother living in Harlem mentioned throughout this book—the question posed in the survey: Do you trust white women a great deal, a good amount, not very much, or not at all? Gordon, like 36 percent of Black women surveyed, said that she did not trust white women very much, acknowledging the complexity: "The reason I didn't say I didn't trust them at all, is mostly layered. I have meaningful, impactful relationships with white women in my life and women who I call friends. I also understand the duality of humanity and system. White women as a system cannot be trusted."[4] For Gordon, this duality is critical because "if you're not careful you can demonize human beings. And this is not about a demonization of a human being, but it is about the demonization and valid critique of how white femininity is dangerous to the social and economic and spiritual livelihood of Black folk."[5]

Gordon's sentiments mirror my own. Some of my earliest friendships were with freckle-faced, redheaded white girls I met at Sunday school. And throughout my life, I have worked, worshipped, studied, lived, loved, friended, valued, and been mentored by white women. And yet, like the chocolate brown color of my skin, distrust remains: a sixth sense, a wariness, and uneasiness.

This lack of trust is grounded in an innate, visceral knowing that was imparted to Black women by their antecedents in resistance to oppression. Like the Black women's inner knowing of Black women discussed in earlier chapters, many Black women have schooled subsequent generations to be cautious, watchful, and vigilant when it comes to white women and their intentions. A Black woman's distrust is her protection. It fosters skepticism and vigilance, which serves as a bulwark against insidious, racialized microaggressions and interactions. Failure to keep one's shield ready risks one's safety. I distrust because I haven't forgotten history or the lived experiences of Black women in the United States. And I believe when it comes down to it, when shit hits the fan, a white woman will choose herself and her whiteness over my Blackness each and every time.

In a four-minute video posted to Instagram, tears streamed down Korey Johnson's face. Her eyes red and puffy, her voice full of despair, "People don't care about Black women, they don't care about Black women's issues."[6]

Johnson is a young Black woman, at the time of the video a one-year graduate of Howard Law School. In recent years, she has become a budding politician and activist according to her active and prolific presence on Instagram and Twitter. As an undergraduate student at Towson University in 2015, Johnson helped to organize rallies against police brutality in Baltimore following the death of Freddie Gray, a young Black man who suffered a fatal spinal cord injury while in police custody.

In the video, which has been viewed on Instagram more than 720,000 times, Johnson shared the disturbing story that evoked tears and distress. She claimed that she and a friend were harassed by a Black man who began to follow them during a recent jog. They sought refuge in a hotel lobby and begged employees to lock the glass doors. According to Johnson, a guest at the hotel, a white woman she did not know, asked about the Black man banging on the doors, trying to gain access to the lobby. "Who let this monkey in?"[7] Johnson alleges the woman continued, "Ya'll clearly know him, is that your baby daddy?"[8]

Crying as she shared the story, Johnson described feeling torn: she was frightened by the Black man who followed her, but she was also very disturbed by the racist words used by the white woman. "For [the white woman] to ask that and to be so racialized in it, I was very upset and very angry."[9]

The video was shared by @tifelomo_ on Twitter. Commenters, particularly Black women, took both offenders to task, but a special vitriol seemed reserved for the white woman described in Johnson's story:

> White women wanna preach feminism so bad but when it comes to black women, they dgaf (@angela_bodley)[10]

> I am a whole feminist but what I've noticed is, it's feminism til it deals with Black women. (@anastasianQveen)[11]

> It is always baffling to me when women don't understand the plight of other women. Smdh (@KEvoLving)[12]

The antagonists in Johnson's story are equally abhorrent and should be held accountable. But I tell this story because it serves as a microcosm of the discord between Black and white women. At a moment when a white woman had an opportunity to see a Black woman as a fellow "sister" in need of help, all she could see was Johnson's Blackness. The Twitter comments reinforce the Marist Poll results that show many Black women in the United States say they do not trust white women. Why should Black women when they never know if or when white women will have their backs?

In one-on-one meetings with me, a former white female coworker professed allyship and friendship. But in strategic upper-management meetings, she regularly downplayed and poked holes in my ideas. In professed solidarity of pay equity, this same coworker (who often boasted about her own income) stressed the importance of women sharing salary details with each other. But then I asked, "How much do you make?" As I waited for her to respond, I wondered if she would be honest and let her guard down with me, the only Black female senior leader on our team? Or would she continue to see me as competition, a threat to her own advancement? I watched and listened to her hem and haw her way through a non-answer. I wasn't surprised by her equivocation. It confirmed what I had already observed and knew to be true about white women. But the most annoying of all my experiences with this same co-worker was that she once asked to touch my hair. My answer? A firm no.

My experiences with this colleague, and other white women, aren't anomalies. When it comes to white women, vigilance is required. In this instance, this means watching my back, keeping a mental file, and discerning when someone does not have my best interest at heart. At work it also means cultivating alliances to minimize vulnerability.

It is impossible to understand the distrust Black women feel toward white women without understanding its inception. And as the Amazon River is long and wide, Black women's distrust of white women is deep and expansive. Augean to cross. Harder still to bridge. Ingrained distrust cultivated by a history of subjugation and betrayals. Betrayals that have traumatized, cementing vigilance. The lack of trust is not about whether white women trust Black women. What is of import here is *why* so many Black women distrust white women.

Black women's distrust began with enslavement. Stephanie E. Jones-Rogers, a historian and professor at the University of California at Berkeley, focuses on gender and US slavery. In her book *They Were Her Property: White Women as Slave Owners in the American South*, Jones-Rogers documented for the first time white women's economic relationships to slavery and "challenge[d] current understandings of white male dominance within southern households and communities in the antebellum era."[13] Jones-Rogers wrote that white women were not simply spectators, but practitioners and beneficiaries of the slave economy.

> [For some white women] slavery was their freedom. They created freedom for themselves by actively engaging and investing in the economy of slavery and keeping African Americans in captivity . . . Women's economic investments in slavery, especially when they used legal loopholes to circumvent legal constraints, allowed them to interact with the state and their communities differently . . . Historians have neglected [to tell the stories of] these women because their behaviors toward and relationships with their slaves do not conform to prevailing ideas about white women and slave mastery . . . slave-owning women not only witnessed the most brutal features of slavery, they took part in them, profited from them, and defended them.[14]

In short, slavery improved the lives of white women and enabled them to circumvent some patriarchal, sexist norms. Beyond the perks of white skin, slavery elevated white womanhood. It ensured an inverse correlation: white women on top, Black women on the bottom. And this was especially significant on the plantation where the white husband/plantation owner raped Black women with impunity, his progeny evident for all to see. Slavery established this contrary relationship, and it remains one of the obstacles hindering the construction of a bridge between Black women and white women.

In 1895, Letitia M. Burwell published a memoir, *A Girl's Life in Virginia Before the War,* that chronicled life in the Antebellum South. The wife of a wealthy, prominent Virginia politician and slave owner, Burwell is indicative of the Victorian ideal. She

dedicated her book to her nieces in defense of their slave-own-
ing heritage. Burwell worried that in a post–Civil War era, her
nieces would believe the "English and American publications"
that described their ancestors as "'cruel slave-owners'; 'inhu-
man retches'; 'southern taskmasters'; [and] 'dealers in human
souls.'"[15]

Throughout the book, Burwell portrayed an idyllic, plea-
sure-filled childhood. And she described the one hundred
enslaved Africans residing on her family's plantation as "lively
and happy." Burwell shared an early memory of vising the
"negro cabins":

> My sister and myself, when very small children, were
> often carried to visit these cabins, on which occasions
> no young princesses could have received from admir-
> ing subjects more adulation. Presents were laid at our
> feet—not glittering gems, but eggs, chestnuts, popcorn,
> walnuts, melons, apples, sweet potatoes, all their "cup-
> boards" afforded, with a generosity unbounded. This
> made us as happy as queens and filled our hearts with
> kindness and gratitude to our dusky admirers. Around
> the cabin doors the young negroes would quarrel as to
> who should be his or her mistress, some claiming me,
> and others my sister.[16]

Even as a child, she understood that the enslaved were her sub-
jects, and she, their queen. Central to Burwell's privileged position is leisure and rest, thanks to the housework performed by
enslaved women. Burwell was proud that their "house servants
were numerous . . . instructed in the branches of household
employment [and] constantly darting about on errands from
the house to the kitchen and the cabins, upstairs and downstairs,

being, indeed, omnipresent and indispensable."[17] The toil of enslaved women gave white women ease and comfort. As noted by scholar and author Sheri Parks, "historically there are situations where the two images are played against each other, certainly during slavery, the weak, fragile, white Victorian ideal of a white woman was only made possible because there were Black women around to do the dirty work. And I mean dirty in all of the ways that we can think of that."[18]

The subornation of Black women enabled Burwell, and women like her, to embody a fantasy for white men: perfect, piteous, and pure, to be honored and adored above all. "All the gentlemen . . . made us feel that we had been put in the world especially to be waited upon by them . . . as some rare and costly statue set in a niche to be admired and never taken down."[19]

A daughter of the south, Burwell was well-acquainted with the horrors of slavery—yet she wrote that their "servants" were never treated poorly. In her memoir, Burwell defends the institution of enslavement and her "noble and virtuous" ancestors who traded in human flesh. Contrived innocence. Gaslighting. Profiting. A trifecta many white women employ today in their interactions with Black folks in general, and Black women in particular.

In the early days of the Abolitionist Movement, some white women advocated for the enslaved. But their support ended when it became clear that the Fourteenth and Fifteenth Amendments to the United States Constitution gave voting rights to Black men before women of any race. Incensed, prominent white suffragists like Elizabeth Cady Stanton showed their true racist colors. To obtain what she believed white women deserved, she betrayed Black women by denigrating and dehumanizing Blackness writ large. White supremacy taking precedence over gender. In a letter to the editor of *The Standard*, on December 26, 1865, Stanton aggressively argued that white women, by virtue of their race, should be enfranchised before Black men:

> The representative women of the nation have done their uttermost for the last thirty years to secure freedom for the negro; and as long as he was lowest in the scale of being, we were willing to press his claims; but now, as the celestial gate to civil rights is slowly moving on its hinges, it becomes a serious question whether we had better stand aside and see "Sambo" walk into the kingdom first . . . Why should the African prove more just and generous than his Saxon compeers?[20]

Historically, white women have proven dangerous for Blackness, irrespective of gender. Black women, along with Black men and boys, have been the target of white women's animus and manipulation. One of the first Black female journalists, Ida B. Wells, investigated lynching in the South during the late 1800s. Through courageous reporting, Wells found that a number of the "alleged cases of assault [against white women] . . . have shown that there was no foundation in fact for the charges . . . [but] no colored man, no matter what his reputation, is safe from lynching if a white woman, no matter what her standing or motive, cares to charge him with insult or assault."[21] Her investigation also discovered that many of the so-called assaults were actually consensual interracial liaisons. And some white women pursued Black men and then cried assault if they were caught.

White women's betrayal of Black women is as American as apple pie. From the Suffrage Movement of the nineteenth century, through the subsequent waves of the Feminist Movements in the twentieth century, to the Women's March in 2017, betrayal hinges on the fact that white women know what it is to be subjugated by white men, to be regulated to second-class citizenry. They have felt the sting of sexism and they have waged battles for parity and equality.

White women have tried to leverage the shared subjugation of patriarchy to establish connection and solidarity with Black women. Tactically, it's a smart move. Aligning with Black women strengthens their own case for gender equality. But invariably what white women want and what Black women need fail to align, with centuries of betrayal hardening distrust.

Fifty years ago, in a column for the *New York Times*, acclaimed novelist and Nobel Prize winner Toni Morrison opined on Black women's hesitancy of joining the women's liberation movement which emerged in the late 1960s:

> What do Black women feel about Women's Lib? Distrust. It is white, therefore suspect. In spite of the fact that liberating movements in the black world have been catalysts for white feminism, too many movements and organizations have made deliberate overtures to enroll blacks and have ended up by rolling them. They don't want to be used again to help somebody gain power—a power that is carefully kept out of their hands. They look at white women and see them as the enemy—for they know that racism is not confined to white men, and that there are more white women than men in this country, and that 53 percent of the population sustained an eloquent silence during times of greatest stress.[22]

Nearly half a century after Morrison called out white women for sustaining "an eloquent silence during times of greatest stress,"[23] Black women, like veteran social justice leader Tamika Mallory, called out white women who voted for Donald Trump—the

Republican nominee who ran a sexist, misogynist, hate-filled campaign—yet ascended to the White House, largely with the help of white female voters.

In 2017, Mallory spoke at the Sydney Opera House where she described a feeling of incredulity, "We didn't think that this man could become president, how did it happen? And we found out that a lot of things happened, but one thing was that 53 percent[24] of white women who voted in the election, voted for Donald Trump. And it was a very, very difficult pill to swallow."[25]

Shortly after the election, Mallory was asked to join a group of white women planning a march, for the day after the inauguration, to protest Trump's presidency. Struggling with feelings of betrayal, Mallory explained to the Sydney audience a deep ambivalence about supporting an endeavor created by white women:

> I get a call to be a part of the Women's March on Washington. And guess what? It was the baby of a white woman . . . And I could have said I won't be involved . . . many women of color said "I will not support this march because the white woman called it and there should have been a march in the white community before calling on us to join [them]. After something so devastating has happened, the betrayal and the wounds are too deep, and we will not support you, we will not be a part of this march." I could have taken that position . . . however, I knew that I could sit on one side of history, or I could be on the right side of history.[26]

According to media reports, the first person to publicly pose the idea for a Women's March on Washington originated with a white grandmother who posted on Facebook on election night 2016: "I think we should march."[27] That post went viral. Shortly thereafter Vanessa Wruble, a white Jewish woman with organizing experience, was brought onboard to plan the March.

A native of Washington, DC, Wruble is a graduate of the elite Sidwell Friends School, attended by several children of US presidents, including Sasha and Malia Obama. Wruble graduated cum laude from Williams College where she studied Women's Issues, Psychology, and Fiction Writing. Wruble also holds two Masters of Arts degrees—from The New School and New York University.

Wruble describes her life work as "producing socially relevant media, political organizing, and redefining the global narrative of modern African culture."[28] According to her LinkedIn page, professional achievements include a stint as a magazine writer, an international correspondent for Al Gore's Current TV, and a humanitarian aid worker in Africa. In 2011, Wruble, along with The Roots drummer Ahmir "Questlove" Thompson, founded OkayAfrica—a digital media platform exploring Africa's film, music, and entertainment culture.

According to *Vogue* magazine, Wruble recognized early on that women of color were not included in the March's planning, so she sent an email to the team, "You need to make sure this is led or centered around women of color, or it will be a bunch of white women marching on Washington . . . That's not okay right now, especially after 53 percent[29] of white women . . . voted for Donald Trump."[30]

New York City born and bred, Mallory comes from a long and rich lineage of activism that began with an ancestor who helped end the enslavement of Black people to her parents who were active in the Civil Rights Movement. The familial legacy of social justice and the shooting death of her son's father irrevocably changed the course of Mallory's life. By the time she was asked to join the Women's March on Washington, Mallory had labored for more than twenty years as a civil rights leader, organizer, and gun control advocate.

Tamika Mallory and Vanessa Wruble are very different women. Their familial backgrounds, lived experiences, and levels of education are disparate. Their class and racial groups distinct. It is important to note these differences as it serves as the foundation of unbridged worldviews and motivations. I posit that the implosion of the Women's March and the group's inability to live up to its intended promise of gender solidarity across intersections of race and class were due to the relationship (or lack thereof) between Mallory and Wruble.

The first Women's March meeting was held in New York City, days after Trump won the election. This inaugural gathering of strangers, which Mallory and Wruble both attended, launched the movement, and revealed deep-seated discord. At first, Wruble was considered a key leader within the March. A daily online Jewish news magazine, *Tablet*, wrote that, "from the very beginning, Vanessa [Wruble] was leading . . . She was the operational leader . . . and she was the linchpin of it all, especially in the early days."[31] The *Tablet* article also alleged that during the first hours of the meeting, Mallory and Carmen Perez, a Chicana feminist organizer, voiced anti-Semitic views:

> . . . as the women were opening up about their backgrounds and personal investments in creating a resistance movement to Trump, Perez and Mallory allegedly first asserted that Jewish people bore a special collective responsibility as exploiters of Black and Brown people—and even . . . claimed that Jews were proven to have been leaders of the American slave trade.[32]

Mallory and Perez denied the allegations. In an interview with *Tablet*, Mallory remembers it differently, "Carmen and I were very clear at that meeting that we would not take on roles as workers or staff, but that we had to be in a leadership position in order for us to engage in the march . . . Other than that, there was no particular conversation about Jewish women, or any particular group of people."[33]

Despite underlying issues exposed at the first meeting, the Women's March on Washington took place on January 21, 2017. It was a huge success, becoming the largest single-day protest in US history. Heralded as the start of a new era, the Women's March galvanized diverse groups of women all over the country to become more politically engaged. During the 2018 midterms, a record number of women ran and won elections across the United States. But behind the scenes of the movement, fault lines were beginning to fracture.

At an official debriefing of the March held at Mallory's apartment in late January 2017, *Tablet* reported that Mallory allegedly told the group "the problem was that there were five white women in the room and only three women of color, and that she didn't trust white women."[34] Evvie Harmon, speaking to a *Tablet* reporter, also claimed that Mallory and Perez began "berating" Wruble for being a Jew. Eventually, Wruble and Mallory both cut ties with the group.

The discord played out publicly with every major news outlet reporting on the controversy. Three points of contention emerged from the expansive news coverage: accusations of anti-Semitism; Mallory's (and others) connection to Nation of Islam leader Louis Farrakhan; and an alleged mismanagement of the organization's sizable donations. I argue that in the fog of controversy and swirl of accusations, the crux of the problem was never properly diagnosed and explained.

As a Black woman, I can look beyond these distractions to the real source of conflict: the power struggle between Mallory, a Black woman, and Wruble, a white woman. (Wruble is Jewish, but she presents as a white woman and is therefore afforded the privileges of white women.) The source of antipathy goes back to the original sin. It is what everything in the United States eventually boils down to: white v. Black, the former enslaver v. the formerly enslaved.

Isabel Wilkerson, author of the *New York Times* bestseller *Caste: The Origins of Our Discontents*, posits that the social order of the United States is based on a caste system that is "the infrastructure of our divisions . . . the architecture of human hierarchy."[35] Wilkerson's construct is predicated on the idea that white folks are at the top and Black folks at the bottom:

> In the American caste system, the signal of rank is what we call race, the division of humans on the basis of their appearance . . . The hierarchy of caste is not about feelings or morality. It is power—which groups have it, and which do not. It is about resources—which caste is seen as worthy of them and which are not, who gets to acquire and control them and who does not. It is about respect, authority, and assumptions of competence—who is accorded these and who is not.[36]

These disparate, yet interconnected social dynamics—caste, race, class—coupled with white supremacy, history, and betrayal, inform the complexities of Black and white women's relationships.

Mallory understood the complexity, "The relationship between women of color and white women is . . . a very strained one . . . particularly [for] Black women as it relates to feminism in our country . . . Black women have not felt that white women have really gone hard if you will for us and our rights."[37] In effect, Mallory articulated why Black women and white women are unbridged.

Given my lived experiences, I proffer that when Mallory walked into that first meeting in November 2016, she had her armor on—ready to protect herself, ready for battle. She knew that the March had been initiated by white women, but she was determined not to be a pawn of tokenism pushed to the background, but to be front and center as a leader, with the authority and respect that entails. It is why Mallory insisted on a leadership position within the March from the very beginning.

As an experienced activist, Mallory is adept at organizing grassroot movements. And she knows the history of social movements in the United States where Black women are often used for their intellect and organizing prowess, but never given credit. Mallory was not going to let that happen to her. History, not vanity nor pride, as some news accounts have suggested, informed her insistence of visibility in title, responsibility, and media appearances.

I gather that Wruble felt validated by her work with OkayAfrica and the credibility conferred by an association with a famous Black man. A *Vogue* magazine article, detailing events leading up to the March, highlighted Wruble's perception that she had experience as "a white person in a Black space."[38] But from my gaze, given European colonization, neocolonization, and imperialism, Wruble's work with OkayAfrica is historically problematic. A white woman promoting a "forward-thinking, nuanced view of Africa"[39] is ridiculous. It is commodified appropriation. It screams impropriety and just feels wrong.

Wruble probably saw her past work as proof of allyship, but to a Black woman like Mallory, or me, it made her more suspect, not less. She likely believed she understood the struggle of Black folks. That is dangerous and presumptuous. And Wruble may have thought that because she pushed for the inclusion of women of color in the initial days of planning, she was trustworthy. Mallory wrote briefly in her 2021 book, *State of Emergency: How We Win in the Country We Built*, about her experiences during the Women's March:

> while I knew the power of the moment, I was also aware that because some in the leadership alongside me weren't as experienced in activism, their potential to be dangerous was high. They had no REAL understanding or commitment to Black life. They thought they could relate, but their connection to our struggle was not rooted in substance. If you haven't dealt with racism that's close to you, you can't adequately address the racism of the world. You don't know what it feels like. You don't know the repercussions of it. You can't even always identify it, at times when it's staring you in the face.[40]

Wruble's likely assumptions and expectation that Mallory would find her trustworthy underscores the dissonance and distance between them. Mallory could not take Wruble at face value. The risk was too high, the work too important. Ultimately, Mallory's vigilance and distrust, coupled with Wruble's naivete and lack of awareness ensured they would remain unbridged.

* * *

In the spring of 2020, a video of George Floyd being killed by the police unleashed a racial reckoning in the United States. The naked cruelty of a public execution reinforced a state-sanctioned disregard for Black lives. And it was in this climate that it was suddenly very popular for white folks to interrogate their complicity in upholding systems of white supremacy.

Antiracist is a term Ibram X. Kendi, director of the Antiracist Research and Policy Center at American University, examined in his book *How to Be an Antiracist*. Kendi defines an antiracist as the opposite of a racist and describes it as "one who is supporting an antiracist policy through their actions or expressing an antiracist idea."[41] An antiracist is about eradicating policies that are racist and have racist outcomes. Published in 2019, Kendi's book became a national bestseller after Floyd's death the following year. And while I respect and honor the choice of Kendi, Black women like Ijeoma Oluo, author of the *New York Times* bestseller *So You Want to Talk About Race*, and those engaged in unconscious bias or diversity and inclusion (D&I) training, I question whether any of it works.

I am of the mindset that the general work—which often includes writing books, teaching new terminology, hosting seminars—of helping white women (and men) unpack their shit should be redirected to the uplift and empowerment of Black women (and men).

The time and energy that some Black women invest in educating white people should be time and energy invested in Black women ascendency. This is especially true today when there is an abundance of easily assessable information. A white woman in the twenty-first century who requires or wants a Black woman to hold her hand as she deconstructs whiteness and wipes away guilty tears is willfully ignorant and lazy. It is not the responsibility of Black women to free white women. But it *is* our responsibility to free ourselves.

To be clear, antiracist work is needed to bring about liberation, but I have learned that there is freedom in accepting what is and what isn't. And history has proven that in the end, white women will do what they have always done, choose whiteness over Blackness, feminism be damned. Antiracism is the new virtue signaling. But does it lead to tangible, positive change or is it simply following the crowd, or a provisional solution?

Glennon Doyle is a white, uber successful mommy blogger turned activist, author, and philanthropist. In her most recent and hugely popular book, *Untamed*, Doyle devotes a chapter to racism and her experience working with Black women on issues of racial equality and white supremacy.

Because Doyle is an influential, cultural voice for white women (with a combined three million [and growing] followers across social platforms), I find it instructive to use her writings to drive home the complexity of Black women's relationships with white women.

In *Untamed*, Doyle takes great pains to demonstrate that she gets the "race conversation." So much so that she admits at the end of the chapter, "I'm afraid to put these thoughts inside a book that will not be in people's hands until a year from now. I know that I will later read this and see racism in it that I cannot see right now."[42]

Doyle wrote that racism should be approached like misogyny, explaining that when a "woman says she wants to work to detox herself of misogyny, she is not labeled a misogynist. It is understood that there is a difference between a misogynist and a person affected by misogyny who is actively working to detox."[43] I take issue with the analysis because it does not recognize and address the complexities of race. White supremacy, the very thing Doyle is desperately trying to purge, is evident in the notion that exorcising racism or misogyny is the same for all women. What Doyle failed to understand is that white women benefit from the former and suffer under the latter. Her logic is faulty because there is no similitude in experience. Black women suffer under both systems of oppression because they intersect *and* operate simultaneously. Oppression for Black women is never "either or." It is always "and."

I wonder how much of this is about protecting Doyle's brand. Doyle has never addressed race in any of her books before. Did the Floyd killing make a difference or was the inclusion of race about being on the right side of the "woke-meter"? I first read *Untamed* more than a year ago and I wrote in the margins of that chapter "I still don't trust you." That was my gut, innate reaction. I don't know if Doyle's efforts to detox white supremacy and racism were successful, but ultimately it is not my focus nor my concern.

In full transparency, I've met Doyle a few times due to connections with a previous employer. We are not friends nor acquaintances, but I think she's sincere, funny, smart, and genuinely wants to help people. In short, I like her. My goal isn't to malign or paint Doyle as disingenuous, but if there is ever going to be a bridge built, truth is required.

Even though I classify Doyle as a "good" person, I was never under the illusion that she was down for the cause. That she would support my Blackness over her whiteness. But I didn't ask her to be or do those things, because I don't need Doyle nor any other white woman to get my plight as a Black woman. What I want is to be treated like the person I am: smart, curious, sincere, and kind, for there to be an appreciation of what makes me, me (and that includes, but is certainly not limited to, the color of my skin).

* * *

Before a civil engineer builds a bridge, she will first ask herself, what is the cost-to-benefit ratio? Typically, bridges are built over obstacles in nature to facilitate commerce and communication. When it comes to determining whether or not to build a bridge, she must understand how the cost-to-benefit ratio compares to the communication and commerce that is already taking place. Another key factor an engineer considers is determining the associated cost to the public in the construction of the bridge. This is determined by understanding how much time it takes to cross the obstacle (like a river) by other means versus how long it would take if a bridge were built. Then an engineer factors in an approximate cost-per-hour for an individual having to take a longer route.

To calculate the total cost of the bridge, the civil engineer also looks at the challenges of building the bridge. For example, even though it is technically possible to bridge the Amazon River, the costs to overcome ecological challenges simply outweigh the benefits. And the fact remains that commerce and communication does happen, though perhaps not quickly, along the Amazon River. Amazonians use boats and ferries to travel along and across the river to purchase goods and visit other communities. Many Amazonians earn a living offering boat tours and river cruises.

The process of cost-to-benefit ratio that civil engineers use is the same process that Black women can use to determine whether to build a bridge over their distrust of white women. The challenges are varied and pose great difficulty: history of slavery, betrayal in the fight for equality, and the continued trauma of everyday microaggressions.

What are the benefits of building a bridge between Black and white women? Are there any benefits? Like the unbridged Amazon River, commerce and communication continues to flow between Black and white women. Many Black women work with white women, buy and sell goods to and from white women, go to school with white women, and have friends who are white women and/or are related to white women.

Black women in the United States do not need to ask, beg, or cajole white women to be our allies. We do not need white women to live happy, fulfilled, successful lives. Do we need to be able to communicate with white women to live productive lives in a pluralistic society? Yes. Do we need to be able to work with them? Of course! Do we want them as customers, to support us, or vote for us? Hell yes! But do we need to trust them unequivocally? I don't think so.

The reality is that there are no absolutes; some Black and white women form deep bonds that supersede obstacles. But for many Black women, a bridge will not fundamentally change the nature of their lives. It is powerful to accept what is. It is powerful to act in one's agency. It is powerful to own one's distrust.

CHAPTER 6

UBUNTU (I AM BECAUSE WE ARE)

A fro-Colombian Francia Márquez chose a powerful campaign slogan for her improbable bid to become Colombia's first Black woman president—*¡Soy Porque Somos!* Translated in English, "I Am Because We Are!" electrified the nation and inspired the marginalized.

Márquez's policy platform opposed multinational corporations, corrupt government, and paramilitary groups and advocated for the poor, the Indigenous, women, and Afro-descendants. After a year of appealing to the electorate, the environmental activist and human rights lawyer turned political neophyte captured the third-largest number of votes during Colombia's 2022 presidential primary. Due to the strong showing, Márquez was selected to be the running mate of Gustavo Petro, presidential frontrunner and former Bogotá mayor. On June 19, 2022, the Petro-Márquez ticket won the election and made history: Márquez became Colombia's first Black vice president. In her acceptance speech in Bogotá, Márquez signaled what was to come, "We women are going to eradicate this country's patriarchy. We're going to fight for the rights of our Mother Earth."[1]

A descendant of enslaved Africans, Márquez grew up sleeping on a dirt floor,[2] mining gold on ancestral lands located in Colombia's southwestern Cauca region. At thirteen, Márquez became an activist when her impoverished village was threatened by a nearby dam project that would have displaced residents and diverted crucial resources. The work to "document the impact . . . on her community and [to seek] reparations"[3] changed the course of Márquez's life, setting her on a path to be a defender of her people.

A single mother and former domestic worker, Márquez garnered international acclaim in 2014 when she led eighty women on a ten-day, 350 kilometer march to Bogotá against illegal mining by multinational corporations. Her efforts successfully pressured the government to remove the illegal miners and equipment from her community. In recognition of her work, Márquez won the Goldman Environmental Prize (sometimes called the environmental Nobel) in 2018.

Despite death threats necessitating full-time bodyguards, Márquez's commitment to justice remains steadfast, "I think our role as Black women has always been the role of resistance . . . we have always been on the front line of facing death and challenging death . . . we have resisted all the ways of oppression but always with hope."[4] Márquez's hope was exemplified in her presidential campaign slogan.

Soy Porque Somos is based on the South African word ubuntu, which means "humanity" or "I am because we are."[5] Ubuntu is derivative of the Zulu phrase "Umuntu ngumuntu ngabantu," which translates to "a person is a person through other people."[6] The late Archbishop Desmond Tutu's exegesis on *ubuntu* is perhaps the best way to understand the African philosophy. Awarded the Nobel Peace Prize in 1984 for his non-violent, anti-Apartheid leadership, Archbishop Tutu wrote eloquently about the capacity of *ubuntu* to bring disparate groups together:

> In Africa, recognition of our interdependence is called ubuntu. It is the essence of being human. It speaks of the fact that my humanity is caught up and is inextricably bound up in yours. I am human because I belong to the whole, to the community, to the tribe, to the nation, to the earth. Ubuntu is about wholeness, about compassion for life . . . In our fragile and crowded world, we can survive only together. We can be truly free, ultimately, only together. We can be human only together.[7]

Archbishop Tutu's unpacking of *ubuntu* is exquisitely poetic: in word choice, imagery, and structure. But more importantly, it offers a clear explanation of the African philosophy's meaning and aspirational tenets. His definition presents an enormous challenge: first, recognize that humanity's fate is indelibly interwoven, fortunes rise and fall in tandem; and second, solving the existential crises of our time requires collaboration, compassion, and a commitment to ending divisive discord.

Ubuntu represents hope. And hope entails patience. It is believing that the desire that is being hoped for will manifest. It is not a passive hope that waits for something to happen, but it is a proactive praxis, one that requires working toward a desire until it is realized. It is this kind of hope that propelled Archbishop Tutu, among others, to convince South Africans to seek reconciliation over retribution at Apartheid's end and compelled Márquez to seek the presidency of Colombia.

The *ubuntu* philosophy is not only a beautiful concept or an empowering campaign slogan, but a key that can unlock doors of liberation. It's adherence to interdependence and belonging provides a path toward building solidarity and community within the Black diaspora, specifically among Afro-descendant women of the trans-Atlantic slave trade.

Transcending borders will require working through differences: in language, culture, and geography; in opinions, perspectives, and ideas; and in lived experiences sullied by white supremacy, colonialism, imperialism, neocolonialism, and patriarchy. For some, differences separate, but for feminist and activist Audre Lorde, difference builds community:

> As women, we have been taught either to ignore our differences, or to view them as causes for separation and suspicion rather than as forces for change. Without community there is no liberation, only the most vulnerable and temporary armistice between an individual and her oppression. But community must not mean a shedding of our differences, nor the pathetic pretense that these differences do not exist.[8]

Liberation for Afro-descendant women of the trans-Atlantic slave trade can be achieved with an adherence to the *ubuntu* philosophy. To manifest *ubuntu*'s ideals that we are all inextricably bound requires a commitment to Lorde's observation that community is best forged and strengthened by differences.

* * *

The Americas, a double continent sandwiched between the Pacific and Atlantic oceans, dominates the Western Hemisphere.

The land connects states, regions, nations, borders, and Afro-descendants of the trans-Atlantic slave trade.

As a Black woman born in the United States, I am well-acquainted with hierarchies based on race, class, and gender. But as a citizen of the world, I am learning to be reflective and cognizant of my own assumptions, biases, and sources of privilege and power that come from living in the Global North.

The positionality of the United States as the world's most dominant economic and military power has fostered an idea of American Exceptionalism, a centering of the country in the minds of its citizens and in the global discourse. This centering, coupled with an educational system that does not teach the truth about slavery, means most Black people in the United States, especially those born here, are unaware of the large number of Black folks residing in Latin America, and the history of how and why that came to be. They also assume that Africans sold during the trans-Atlantic slave trade were sent primarily to North America. But those assumptions are misinformed. Correcting assumptions is crucial to forging deeper ties with all Black women who are descendants of the transnational slave trade.

The United Kingdom did not hold a monopoly on the slave economy fueled by the triangular trade routes between Europe, West Africa, and the New World. Europeans from Spain, Portugal, France, and the Netherlands also enthusiastically participated in the lucrative business of selling African bodies. For centuries, they robbed, plundered, and murdered their way across the New World in service to their monarchs and greed. The seeds of this shameful history—strife between Black and white, oppressed and the oppressor—have borne strange fruit. Not only in the United States, but throughout the Americas.

As early as the sixteenth century, Portugal and Spain became the first European countries to embark on slave voyages from Africa to the Americas. In fact, the first "20 and odd Negroes"[9] to arrive at an English colony in 1619 were not headed there. English pirates intercepted a Portuguese vessel enroute to Mexico. The pirates stole as many Africans as they could fit on their ships, sailed north to Virginia, and sold them for food and supplies.

According to David Eltis and David Richardson, historians and purveyors of the Trans-Atlantic Slave Database,[10] between the sixteenth and nineteenth centuries, European traders captured and transported approximately 12.5 million Africans to the New World. Of the estimated 10.7 million who survived the brutal, inhumane journey known as the Middle Passage, over 90 percent disembarked in colonies in the Caribbean and South America. Brazil received the majority of the enslaved Africans (4.8 million) and the United States received 450,000 Africans. These details matter, not to absolve colonies or countries that did not take in as many slaves, but to broaden the notion of where most enslaved Africans were taken and where many of their descendants live today.

The late Dr. Colin Palmer defined a diaspora as an "organic process involving movement from an ancestral land, settlement in new lands, and sometimes renewed movement and resettlement elsewhere."[11] A historian and professor, Palmer identified five major African diasporic streams over the last hundred thousand years. The fourth diaspora covers the forced migration of the trans-Atlantic slave trade. Even though the descendants of the trans-Atlantic slave trade number in the millions and live all over the world, Palmer posited that they are:

> United by a past based significantly but not exclusively upon "racial" oppression and the struggles against it; and who, despite the cultural variations and political and other

divisions among them, share an emotional bond with one another and with their ancestral continent; and who also, regardless of their location, face broadly similar problems in constructing and realizing themselves.[12]

The emotional bond between Afro-descendant women of the trans-Atlantic slave trade is due in large part to the same systems of oppression—identified by bell hooks as "imperialist white supremacist capitalist patriarchy"[13]—that impact Black women throughout the Americas. The emotional bond is also based on the fact that Afro-descendant women are largely leading the battles for social justice. This bond is not predicated on proximity, and it has not been weakened by the passage of time.

There are approximately two hundred million people who identify as being of African descent living in the Americas. In the United States, 46.8 million people self-identified as Black, making up roughly 14 percent of the population. In Canada, the Black population accounts for 3.5 percent (1.3 million people) of the total population. And a World Bank report estimates that one in four (133 million) Latin Americans identify as people of African descent.[14] Of that total, 91 percent of Afro-descendants are concentrated in Venezuela and Brazil (which is second only to Nigeria in the number of Afro-descendants).

Even though transnational intersectionalities ensure that some lived experiences between Afro-descendant women transcend borders, Palmer pointed out that "scholars must be careful not to homogenize the experiences of the diverse peoples of the modern diaspora . . . there are fundamental differences born of the societal context, the times, the political, economic, and 'racial' circumstances."[15] While colonization and imperialism have centered Black identity throughout the Americas, how it shows up is far from homogenous.

* * *

I simply adore my friend's mother. A Dominican octogenarian with sparkling eyes, she is saucy, funny, and vibrant. At a function a few years ago, my friend's mother and I greeted each other with a warm hug. As she pulled back from the embrace, she looked directly into my eyes and said, "I always wanted a daughter with your darker skin. You're so beautiful."

Taken aback, I managed to stammer out "thank you?" But to my ears the "you" sounded strangely high pitched, proof of my confusion and discomfort. Phenotypically white, she has pale skin and eyes, a straight nose, and shoulder length (albeit dyed) blond hair. While her husband has a darker complexion, her children, including my friend, inherited their mother's fair skin and features.

I was acutely aware that her words were laden with subtext and meaning. But I also knew I did not understand the cultural nuances of race and ethnicity in the Dominican Republic to engage in conversation. And in that moment, I thought, if a white woman had said the same thing, my reaction would have been swift, sharp, and severe.

Like most people born in the United States, my idea of race has been molded and shaped by the one-drop rule. The de facto standard that a single drop of Black blood is all it takes for someone to be deemed Black was promulgated during the colonial period to ensure any baby born of an African woman would be enslaved. It was codified into law during the early twentieth century and upheld as recently as 1985 when a Louisiana court ruled that Susie Guillory Phipps could not change her race from "colored" to "white" on her birth certificate because of a Black, enslaved great-great-great-great-grandmother in her bloodline.[16]

University of Oregon associate professor and Afro-Dominican Ana-Maurine Lara has written extensively about Black identity formation across the Americas:

> In the Latin American context, rather than quantifying race by one drop, Iberian laws connoted gradations of racial categorization based on specific mixtures of blood. This simultaneously obscured *negritud* and made blackness central to *Criollo* identity all at once, in that the official number of "*negros*" decreased, while the number of "*mestizos, pardos, mulatos, zambos,*" etc. increased. In the United States, with the one-drop rule, whiteness became central to racial identity formation, and polarized people into essential categories. It is this tension between centrality and essentialism that plays out when an Afro-Latina body walks through spaces in the United States.[17]

Born in the Dominican Republic, but raised in the United States, Lara moved back to Santo Domingo as an adult. She expected the move to be permanent, but when she couldn't find work, she was back in the United States within a matter of months, "[it] had everything to do with my perceived race and class. At the time I had dreadlocks . . . No one would hire me because of my 'appearance.'"[18]

According to Lara, the racial discrimination she experienced in the Dominican Republic can be partly attributed to *anti-haitianismo*[19]—a racist, nationalist conception of Haitians that centers on their African ancestry and resentment of Haiti's short-lived nineteenth-century occupation of its neighboring country:

> "Blackness" in the Dominican context is equated to Haitian-ness, and Haitian-ness is equated with numerous assumptions

about the social value and worth of dark-skinned people. These assumptions are embedded in the social, political, and economic structures of the nation, and limit the livelihoods of dark-skinned people across the country.[20]

The formation of racial identity in the Dominican Republic, and throughout Latin America, is shaped further by beliefs of who is and who isn't Black. "Black as an identity belonged to people of African descent born in the United States, and that identity evoked specific cultural values, norms, and points of view."[21]

Even though Lara's experience can't speak for all Latinos in the diaspora, her analysis provides useful insight into the ways Latinos conceive of the Black identity. According to Lara, in Latin America, there is no difference between Black and Black American, they are one and the same. If Blackness is indicative of the United States, then it makes sense that an African descendant in Venezuela would not see herself as Black. But just as important, Lara demonstrates how differences in Black identity formation can cause underlying tension. While I may believe that race is essentially binary (black/white) and take a great deal of pride in being Black, for an Afro-descendant woman in the Caribbean, the Black identity may not be central to her self-conception.

Lara's historical and social analysis of Blackness in the Dominican Republic and personal anecdotes provided the context for examining the interaction I had with my friend's Dominican-born mother, a woman who is likely familiar with the racial tensions existent between Haitians and Dominicans.

Given the higher status afforded those who look white in the Dominican Republic, my sense is that the attention paid to my skin color was more about seeing me as somehow different from Haitians because I was born in the United States. This episode is analogous to when a white person in the United States says to a Black person, "you're not like other Black people" as if it were a compliment. Additionally, my skin tone is closer to mocha brown and perhaps she would not have said she wanted a daughter with my skin color if I were darker. Needless to say, the objectification lets me know that she likely sees Blackness as otherness and less than, given the history of *anti-haitianismo*.

As the literary historian Henry Louis Gates, Jr., points out in his book *Black in Latin America*, the meaning of Blackness and the naming of skin color vary in each of the six countries he studied: Brazil, Mexico, Peru, Dominican Republic, Haiti, and Cuba. Still, Gates discovered "that persons of the seemingly 'purest' or 'unadulterated' African descent disproportionately occupy the very bottom of the economic scale in each of these countries. In other words, the people with the darkest skin, the kinkiest hair, and the thickest lips tend to be overrepresented among the poorest members of society."[22] The reality of colorism and racism throughout Latin America demonstrate the pervasiveness of white supremacy, colonialism, and capitalism.

In the same way a virus infects a host cell, so too has the legacy of the trans-Atlantic slave trade infected the Americas. It may show up in Jamaica as colorism, Colombia as illegal mining of gold, Honduras as the seizure of ancestral lands, in the United States as gentrification, or in Canada as police brutality, but it all comes from the same infectious microbe.

Much of the discussion in this chapter has focused on the southern countries in the Western hemisphere, due to the vast number of Afro-descendants that reside there, but Canada is not immune to the sickness of racism.

In the 1600s, slavery was a common practice in the colony of New France, the first major settlement in what is now Canada. Out of approximately 4,200 enslaved people in New France at the peak of slavery, the majority were Indigenous people and roughly 1,400 were Africans. Although slavery operated on a much smaller scale when compared to other American colonies, the history of enslavement continues to negatively impact the daily lives of Black Canadians.

In 2021, the Black Canadian National Survey found that 70 percent of Black Canadians face racism regularly or from time to time, compared to Indigenous people (49 percent), other non-white Canadians (48 percent), and White Canadians (18 percent).[23] Seventy-eight percent of Black Canadians think racism is a severe problem and 70 percent experience racism in Canada on a regular basis. The results also showed that an overwhelming number of Black Canadians reported that racism is an issue in the workplace (96 percent) and racism is a problem in healthcare (91 percent). In an interview with CityNews Toronto, Beverly Bain, professor of Women and Gender Studies at the University of Toronto Mississauga, said that Canada has a grim history when it comes to its treatment of Black people, but she added, "Black people have always resisted oppression."[24]

* * *

Discovering the expansive activism of Black women throughout the Americas is like reading about the exploits of the Hall of Faith heroes described in scripture. Instead of protagonists like Sarah and Rahab, who by faith achieved the impossible, there are Afro-descendant women who by grit, "a firmness of mind or spirit,"[25] are breaking barriers and shattering glass ceilings. Grit was explored by Angela Duckworth in her *New York Times* bestseller, *Grit: The Power of Passion and Perseverance*:

. . . grit is about having what some researchers call an "ultimate concern"—a goal you care about so much that it organizes and gives meaning to almost everything you do. And grit is holding steadfast to that goal. Even when you fall down. Even when you screw up. Even when progress toward that goal is halting or slow.[26]

The "ultimate concern" for Black women in the Americas is not fame or fortune, but the liberation of their people. The "ultimate concern" is life over death: access to affordable food, housing, healthcare, and livable wages. The "ultimate concern" is to create a society where everyone is treated equally, where life abounds, humanity is valued, and the planet is protected. Black women descendants of the trans-Atlantic slave trade are laboring to bring such a world to fruition.

By grit, Afro-Canadian Robyn Maynard is working to shed light on anti-Black racism and to dispel the myth that Canada is post-racial and void of discrimination. A feminist, writer, activist, and educator, Maynard argues that the "invisibility of Black life in Canada has meant that most people . . . are not aware that slavery existed in Canada for over 200 years."[27]

With a background in community activism and advocacy, Maynard is the author of the bestseller *Policing Black Lives: State Violence in Canada from Slavery to the Present*. By grit, Maynard links slavery to present-day oppression,

Black people are ten times more likely than whites to be killed by the police and are incarcerated at a rate of over three times their make-up in the general population . . . the police killings of Chevranna Abdi, Bony Jean-Pierre, and Andrew Loku—all Black—and the recent handcuffing of a six-year old [sic] Black girl in her elementary school are not isolated phenomena, but outgrowths of centuries-old practices of the surveillance and punishment of Black populations.[28]

By grit, Afro-Honduran Miriam Miranda has labored for more than three decades to protect the legal, economic, social, and land rights of Garifuna communities. The Garifuna are an Afro-Indigenous group, proud descendants of West Africans who escaped enslavement in the early 1600s. Today, the Garifuna are spread throughout Latin America with approximately a hundred thousand living in Honduras. By grit, Miranda became the leader of the Black Fraternal Organization of Honduras which advocates on behalf of the Garifuna's "longstanding struggle to save their ancestral land from drug traffickers, palm oil magnates and tourism developers aided by corrupt government officials and institutions."[29] In 2019, when over a dozen Garifuna activists were killed, Miranda refused to be silenced, warning that her people faced extermination.

By grit, Miranda has endured imprisonment and death threats because she believes that Black women like herself, "are at the forefront of the struggles for our rights, against racial discrimination, for the defense of our commons and our survival. We're at the front not only with our bodies but also with our force, our ideas, our proposals. We don't only birth children, but ideas and actions as well."[30]

By grit, the late human rights activist Afro-Brazilian Marielle Franco, thirty-eight, died a martyr, fighting for the rights of the marginalized. Elected to Rio de Janeiro's city council in 2016, Franco was the only LGBTQ Black female representative and one of seven women on the fifty-one-seat council. By grit, Franco was outspoken and critical of the "police's often deadly raids in densely populated shantytowns, or favelas, and denounced paramilitary groups run by retired and off-duty police known as milícias."[31]

On March 14, 2018, Franco hosted a panel at *Casa das Pretas* (The Black Women's House). It was later described as an empowering evening that attracted young Black women activists, writers, entrepreneurs, intellectuals, and musicians. On the way home from the event, a vehicle pulled up alongside Franco's car in downtown Rio de Janeiro. A gunman fired nine bullets. Four of them hit Franco in the head and three hit her driver. Both were instantly killed.

Franco's death galvanized millions of Black Brazilian women and members of the LGBTQ community to pressure the government to arrest those responsible for her death. By grit, dozens of Black women inspired by Franco ran "for statewide office in Brazil in 2018. Rio de Janeiro elected three Black women state representatives, and São Paulo sent Brazil's first Black trans woman to the state congress."[32]

Four hundred kilometers west of Rio de Janeiro is São Paulo, the heart of Brazil's financial center. It's home to another gritty Afro-Brazilian woman. In 2019, Janice Ferreira da Silva, known as "Preta" (Black woman) Ferreira, was imprisoned for 109 days in Santana Women's Prison. A housing rights activist and coordinator of the Homeless Movement of Downtown São Paulo (MSTC), Ferreira was arrested on charges of extortion for allegedly coercing residents into paying fees to live in squats.

As reported by *Zora*, an online publication that aims to amplify the voices of Black women, Ferreira's "movement help[ed] vulnerable people acquire housing by leading occupations of abandoned buildings in São Paulo. Her work to guarantee disadvantaged people safe, affordable, centrally located housing—though a constitutional right in Brazil—had been criminalized by local political actors."[33]

By grit, Ferreira rejected normative roles for women: "I was born in this sexist, racist, oppressive republic. The fact that I am a Black woman and influence other people to demand their constitutional rights is outrageous to them . . . They chose the role I have to play, doing dishes, cooking food. And that's not my role."[34] By grit, Ferreira persevered until she was freed from prison, "the slogan of her movement evolv[ing] from *Preta Livre!* (Free Preta) to *Pretas Livres!* (Free All Black Women)."[35]

A trademark of gritty Afro-descendent women in the Americas is a collective inner knowing. And that knowing *knows* Black women are at the nexus of activism and progress.

* * *

I have argued in this chapter that while there is much that separates Afro-descendant women of the trans-Atlantic slave trade, there is also much that unites them. I've shared how Afro-descendant women are on the frontlines, leading in the on-going battle for liberation. The time is ripe to forge new and strengthen existing transnational alliances.

Transnational feminism theory and practice offers a way to think about alliances that transcend borders. The foremost objective of transnational feminism "is to destabilize notions that women around the world share the same types of experiences, oppressions, forms of exploitation, and privileges; [it] explores differences and inequalities between women, such as different priorities and ways of understanding gender issues and different ways of conceptualizing agency."[36] This idea ensures that the voices of all women are heard and valued by giving equal weight to women, regardless of whether they are from the Global North or Global South. It is the idea that women, irrespective of cultural norms, have their own ideas about how to address local inequalities and that those ideas should be heard, honored, and respected.

Transnational feminism also endeavors to "foster transnational solidarity and collaboration between feminists who are from different countries or the diaspora and who value difference as a foundation for activism."[37] It expands on the basic tenets of intersectionality, "emphasizing global structural and historical factors such as economic exploitation and oppressive forces associated with colonialism, imperialism, extreme forms of capitalism, structural racism, and gendered racism, as well as other forms of globalization that reinforce the dominance of Northern world regions."[38] A framework that honors the contributions, thoughts, and inputs of each person supports collaboration and allyship-building based on shared objectives.

An early scholar of transnational feminism, Syracuse University professor Chandra Mohanty pioneered the idea of transnational solidarity:

> I define solidarity in terms of mutuality, accountability, and the recognition of common interests as the basis for relationships among diverse communities. Rather than assuming an enforced commonality of oppression, the practice of solidarity foregrounds communities of people who have chosen to work and fight together. Diversity and difference are central values here—to be acknowledged and respected, not erased in the building of alliances.[39]

Legendary activist, feminist, and scholar Angela Y. Davis is one of the best examples of fidelity to international solidarity. Like Marvel's *Black Panther*'s Shuri, the inventive Princess of Wakanda, Davis is a superhero for dozens of progressive Black women throughout the Americas. Solidarity, for Davis, "is absolutely essential. I don't think we can accomplish anything really that will move us in a progressive direction without . . . international solidarity."[40]

For decades Davis has embodied her own definition, by sharing advice, support, and her connections with fellow Afro-descendant activists in Latin America and Canada. Examples of Davis's international solidarity are exemplified in decades of laboring alongside Afro-Brazilian feminist and anthropologist Lélia Gonzalez in the 1980s and her 2019 visit to the home of activist Preta Ferreira (who was on house arrest in São Paulo following her release from prison). When Afro-Colombian Francia Márquez traveled to the United States for the first time in 2010, she had the opportunity to meet Davis in San Francisco: "For me she is an Afro-descendant woman who has inspired me. I have also known of the anti-racist struggle here for many years and that she has been key in that struggle."[41]

The genesis of Davis's steadfast commitment to international solidarity is rooted in the global "free Angela Davis" campaign. Davis had been charged with murder, kidnapping, and criminal conspiracy when a deadly, failed attempt to free prisoners led to a shoot-out outside a California courthouse in 1970. Although she was not present during the shooting, Davis was alleged to have purchased the guns. She served roughly eighteen months in jail and was acquitted in June 1972 after her case drew the attention of the international press. Davis has never forgotten the support of the international community and its role in securing her freedom.

Davis connects the founding of the Black Panther Party in 1966 and the immediate "chapters in Brazil, New Zealand and Palestine, all over the world"[42] as an example of international solidarity and the importance of being in communication across borders.

Essential to international solidarity is open, consistent communication that fosters respect and true understanding. Walter Rodney—Guyanese scholar and activist in the anticolonial revolution and Jamaica's Black Power movements—published a seminal book in 1969, *The Groundings with My Brothers*. Rodney defines "groundings" as a process of centering communication that will serve to build Black people's solidarity:

> I was prepared to go anywhere that any group of Black people were prepared to sit down to talk and listen. Because, that is Black Power, that is one of the elements, a sitting down together to reason, to "ground" as the Brothers say . . . the new understanding is that Black Brothers [and Sisters] must talk to each other.[43]

A part of the ancient African tradition of oral storytelling, "grounding" offers a rich opportunity for diasporic connections. Scholars and activists have identified approaches that can serve to effectuate change across borders based on shared goals and objectives that are made possible by the forming of deep connections. Introduced by scholars Margaret E. Keck and Kathryn Sikkink, transnational activism networks enable the mobility of information, "to help create new issues and categories, and to persuade, pressurize, and gain leverage over much more powerful organizations and governments. Activists in networks try not only to influence policy outcomes, but to transform the terms and nature of the debate."[44]

The success of transnational activism networks is evident in the Black Lives Matter (BLM) movement. Since BLM launched in 2013, it has grown into a member-led global network of more than forty chapters. From the United Kingdom, France, and Canada to Australia, Mexico, and Brazil, BLM protests have occurred all over the world, transforming the debate around police brutality, the criminal justice system, and the conditions of Black and Brown people not just in the United States, but all

over the global. In an article appearing in the *Black Scholar* journal, a connection was made between BLM and the 2018 killing
of Brazilian activist and politician Marielle Franco:

> Thus, we have come full circle. While there are explicit
> and implicit connections between the U.S. Movement for
> Black Lives and Brazil, the current movement against anti-
> black genocide in Brazil is an organic extension of gen-
> erations of resistance against anti-black state violence in
> Brazil. Marielle was one of a cohort of black queer women
> leading the global fight to end anti-black state-sponsored
> terror. She had even committed herself to learning English
> through intensive readings of the works of black feminist
> scholars such as Audre Lorde, bell hooks, Angela Y. Davis,
> among others, as a concrete way to link Brazilian move-
> ments to ideas and struggles for freedom and justice taking
> place around the world. If we recognize the Movement for
> Black Lives as a global coalition to fight against anti-black
> state violence, then Marielle Franco is yet another martyr
> for this global movement.[45]

Black women across the Americas have a unique opportunity
to be in solidarity in a strategic way that would prove mutually
beneficial.

* * *

There is a longstanding, rich history within the Black diaspora
of collaboration, partnership, and communication. And in a
global, digital world, opportunities for information sharing and
solidarity building have never been easier. But the work of creating and sustaining transnational networks has historically been

the vanguard of scholars and activists. As someone who sits outside of the academe, I argue that the knowledge building of Black feminist scholars and activists in transnational networking needs to be disseminated to Black women as a whole.

Many Black women in the United States do not have a transnational awareness of African-descended women, of the trans-Atlantic slave trade, who also experience intersectional oppression and are also leading the charge to dismantle these systems. American Exceptionalism fosters a myopic, self-centered, Global North worldview that disregards less affluent countries. This lack of awareness is damaging to all African-descended Black women because it handicaps the power derived through transnational solidarity and mobilization. While alliances across borders is happening to some degree, an amplification and expansion of these alliances is critical. Black feminist scholar Patricia Hill Collins wrote about the vital connection between the liberation of Black women in the United States and transnational alliances, "Black women's empowerment involves revitalizing U.S. Black feminism as a social justice project organized around the dual goals of empowering African American women and fostering social justice in a transnational context."[46]

Building transnational alliances that advance shared goals of liberation is work that has to move beyond the Ivory Tower or even a protest march. In the same way that Septima Poinsette Clark, the Civil Rights activist discussed in chapter four, developed a curriculum that taught Black folks in the South how to overcome racist policies that kept them from voting. I argue that Black women scholars and activists should follow Clark's example and travel around the country, or host virtual sessions, that teach Black women the power and necessity of transnational alliances and international solidarity.

We can also include women from the Global South by inviting them to join these virtual sessions or bring them to the United States and into classrooms, rallies, or other spaces. And folks in the United States can visit Afro-descendant women in their countries and engage in their spaces. The goal is for Black women in the United States to learn that they are not alone in the battle for liberation. They will learn of women like Afro-Colombian Francia Márquez who believes:

> Everyone comes into this world with a purpose. Everyone has a reason for being. In my heart, fighting for the rights of Black communities is my reason: for my rights as an Afro-descendant woman, for our territories and for our lives. I believe I was created for this reason. I don't know if I'll die tomorrow or when I'll die, but I'm at peace. . .[47]

Together, in solidarity, in the spirit of *ubuntu,* true liberation, true community will be possible for all Black women.

In the words of Archbishop Desmond Tutu, "we can survive only together. We can be truly free, ultimately, only together. We can be human only together."[48]

CHAPTER 7
LOVE OF POWER

I was a lioness on the hunt.
Waiting in the dark.
Ready to pounce.

During the mid-2010s, I worked for a digital content site boasting one of the largest online audiences in the world, driving billions of video views each year.

At the time, a white male colleague and I co-led the news video team. I was not happy with the arrangement. Not because I had an issue with his abilities—he was intelligent and an asset to the organization—but I believe teams are more effective when they have one clear leader. And between the two of us, I was stronger at running teams.

I spoke with our boss at least two times about my concerns. A year later, the news division realigned under another senior vice president. I had a new boss. And I formed a new strategy.

I was a lioness on the prowl.
So, I did what lions do.

And I pounced.

First, I secured the support of senior leaders in the news division. Then I met with the new SVP and pitched myself as the head of the video team. Following our meeting, the SVP met with senior leaders and they affirmed that I was perfect for the role. That sealed the deal.

I share my story as a testament to my power—fully aware that it is radical for a Black woman to recognize her power and admit to using it. But I am not alone. According to the national survey I conducted in partnership with Marist Poll, when Black women were asked whether success in life is pretty much determined by forces outside of their control or whether everyone has it in their own power to succeed, three in four Black women (75 percent) believe that everyone has it in their own power to succeed, whereas just 25 percent believe success is determined by outside forces. That tells me Black women are aware of their power and in their ability to exercise power for their benefit.

The survey is representative of my lived experiences. When I met with the colleague who had co-run the video team with me, he admitted that he didn't know the position was open. But it wasn't. I saw an opportunity to actualize the desired role: success was within my own power to wield and I acted.

Power is a learned skill. It took years, countless failures, and life experiences to discover that power is necessary. And if power is necessary, there is an art to its acquisition. And that requires prudence, patience, and prescience.

True mastery of power is wielding it like a Black woman. That happens when normative archetypes of power—built and cemented in white supremacist patriarchy—is summarily rejected. Power, when used appropriately and motivated by love, is a tool Black women can use to determine the quality of their lives and to remold society.

Before power can be effectively employed, it is essential to understand power: its nature, function, and complexity. Power is nebulous. It is invisible, intangible. An interplay of wants and needs. Foolish to ignore but wise to respect. From Socrates and Plato to Weber and Foucault, a few dozen white male, Western philosophers have held power over the very construct of power. White supremacy and patriarchy are imbued in power's epistemology.

The most straightforward definition was developed by German sociologist Max Weber, "[power is the] ability to control others, events, or resources; to make happen what one wants to happen in spite of obstacles, resistance, or opposition."[1]

* * *

It's 1981. The studio is sparse and dark. A low rectangular oak table separates the interviewer and interviewee. Asking the questions, André Berten, a professor at Belgium's Catholic University of Louvain. Answering the questions, Michel Foucault, a renowned French philosopher and historian.

Wearing a dark gray suit, arms propped on knees, hands tightly clasped, Foucault leans forward and looks intently at Berten. "Power," he explains haltingly in English a definition that differs from Weber, "is a relation, it isn't a thing. It is a relation between individuals, a relation which can direct or determine another's behavior . . . according to strategies."[2] Foucault examined the functionality of power. He introduced the term "disciplinary power," "a form of power that tells people how to act by coaxing them to adjust themselves to what is 'normal.' It is power in the form of correct training . . . Discipline works

[to] produce obedient people."[3] To illustrate disciplinary power, Foucault turned to the Panopticon, a concept developed by eighteenth-century philosopher Jeremy Bentham.

The Panopticon is a prison system where power is woven into its architectural design. At the center of the Panopticon is a tower. The tower is the guard's command center. Circling the perimeter of the tower is a ring-shaped structure composed of inmate cells.

The cell wall that faces the inner tower is made of glass, ensuring inmates are always visible, heightening their awareness of surveillance. The walls of the center tower facing the inmates are also made of glass. But with one important distinction—a light shines inside the tower. This works as a backlight preventing inmates from knowing when or if they are being watched.

In his book *Discipline & Punish: The Birth of the Prison*, Foucault explained, "[the inmate] is seen, but he does not see; he is the object of information, never a subject in communication . . . And this invisibility is a guarantee of order."[4] In time, prisoners become a "principle of [their] subjection"[5] by curbing their own behavior, reinforcing a power structure that affirms the automatic functioning of power and compliance.

Foucault's theory of disciplinary power extends beyond the prison walls—illuminating "power relations in terms of [the] everyday life."[6] Traffic laws serve as an example. When approaching a red stoplight, drivers automatically stop. Why? The driver never knows who is watching. On the oft chance there is a police officer nearby or a red-light camera installed in the stoplight, the driver will self-correct and follow the rules to avoid the discipline of a ticket. That is disciplinary power—constant surveillance determining normality, demanding conformity, "the existence of a whole set of techniques and institutions for measuring, supervising and correcting the abnormal."[7]

Disciplinary power engenders docility in the pursuit of obedience and control. Like the prisoners of the Panopticon, Black women are uniquely visible. Their hair, their skin, their bodies, their colloquialisms, their mannerism, their dope*ness* subjected to extreme surveillance. A surveillance that seeks to curb behavior. Many Black women have stories of being watched and followed when navigating public spaces. I have certainly felt monitored as the only Black woman executive in corporate settings. Surveillance normalizes hypervisibility. And invisibility. And erasure. Surveillance normalizes submission, sometimes against one's interest, to power structures.

Black women have learned to question their inherent power. If they think they have power, they question whether they have a right to power. If they think they have a right to power, they question whether they know how to use it, and if they get through all of that, they question whether it is bad to pursue power itself. I want to destroy the normalization of powerlessness. It is not normal for Black women to relinquish power or to accept erasure. To forgo power is to inhibit an ability to create meaningful, lasting change.

The exercise of power, according to Nobel Laureate Bertrand Russell, is an expression of humanity. His theory credits power as the spark that leads to societal change. And a "strong love of power"[8] results in "influence on the course of events."[9] Conversely, a lack of this love renders one impotent, unable to have an impact, "the men [or women] who cause social changes are, as a rule, men [or women] who strongly desire to do so. Love of power, therefore, is a characteristic of the men [or women] who are causally important . . . love of power is the chief motive producing [change]."[10] Russell asserts that societal or personal change will not happen without wielding power. And wielding power will not happen with loving power.

Social theorist and professor Patricia Hill Collins is one of the preeminent thinkers and scholars on race, class, and gender. In the classic twentieth century *Black Feminist Thought: Knowledge, Consciousness, and the Politics of Empowerment,* Collins does what no other white philosopher could or cared to do—interrogate power via a Black woman's lens. Collins's work demonstrates how Black women can exercise power and not oppress others in the process. By centering Black feminist thought and activism in the epistemology of power and empowerment, Collins explains how the intersectionality of systemic oppressions (what she terms the matrix of domination) is organized into four domains of power: structural, disciplinary, hegemonic, and interpersonal.

The structural domain of power examines how the organization of US social institutions, including but not limited to, "policies and procedures of the . . . legal system, labor markets, schools, the housing industry, banking, insurance, the news media . . . have worked to disadvantage"[11] Black women and keep them in subordination.

The disciplinary domain of power builds on the work of Foucault. Collins argues that the use of disciplinary power grew in significance with the expansion of bureaucracy in modern social organizations. She examines how disciplinary power limits every stage and aspect of a Black woman's life:

> Bureaucracies, regardless of the policies they promote, remain dedicated to disciplining and controlling their workforces and clientele. Whether the inner-city public schools that many Black girls attend, the low-paid jobs in the rapidly growing service sector that young Black women are increasingly forced to take, the culture of social welfare bureaucracy that makes Black mothers and

children wait for hours, or the "mamified" work assigned
to Black women professionals, the goal is the same—creating quiet, orderly, docile, and disciplined populations of
Black women. [12]

Despite bureaucratic policies' reliance on disciplinary power to
curb the progress of Black women, Collins asserted that Black
women's resistance to these polices can limit their effectiveness.

Another aspect of the domain of power identified by Collins
is interpersonal and it "functions through routinized, day-to-
day practices of how people treat one another."[13] The interpersonal domain requires introspection and humility. It encourages
Black women to take a look at "that piece of the oppressor which
is planted deep within each of us."[14] The interpersonal domain
of power challenges how one's "thoughts and actions uphold
someone else's subordination."[15] In the discourse and use of
power, it is critical that Black women are mindful of potential
impacts on other marginalized groups. Black women cannot get
free by imprisoning others.

The hegemonic domain of power, as discussed by Collins,
manipulates ideology, culture, and consciousness. It is a method
employed by dominant groups to maintain their power by "creating and maintain[ing] a popular system of 'commonsense'
ideas that support their right to rule."[16] The hegemonic domain
of power links all of the domains of power by justifying their
practices. The notion of the "right to rule" (as in the white man's
right to rule) is predicated on hegemonic ideologies that serve to
perpetuate stereotypes and false narratives about Black women.
Powered by the mass media, "the significance of the hegemonic
domain of power lies in its ability to shape consciousness via
the manipulation of ideas, images, symbols, and ideologies."[17]
Black women can combat stereotypes and hegemonic domain

of power by holding on to the inner knowing described in chapter one. It is a knowing that values, believes in, and fosters self-worth and self-love.

* * *

In Black folks' battle for equality and freedom, power has never been the end goal. The Abolitionist Movement was about eradicating slavery. The Civil Rights Movement was about the right to vote and abolishing Jim Crow. The Black Power Movement was about group solidarity and amassing power separate from white America. Black Feminism is about understanding how intersecting oppressions impact lived experiences. And Black Lives Matter is largely about ending violent policing and criminalization.

Though dreams inspire, rage is cathartic.

Power will get us to the Promised Land.

In 1967, Dr. Martin Luther King Jr. published the book *Where Do We Go From Here: Chaos or Community?* That same year Stokely Carmichael, the leader of the Student Nonviolent Coordinating Committee (SNCC), also published a book, *Black Power: The Politics of Liberation.* Both were leaders in the Civil Rights Movement. Both had committed their lives to the freedom of Black people. But when it came to power, King and Carmichael (who later changed his name to Kwame Ture) were on opposing sides of an ideological and generational schism.

In *Where Do We Go From Here*, King recounted a defining moment during the Meredith Mississippi Freedom March in 1966:

At a huge mass meeting that night, which was held in a city park, Stokely mounted the platform and after arousing the audience with a powerful attack on Mississippi justice, he proclaimed: "What we need is black power." Willie Ricks, the fiery orator of SNCC, leaped to the platform and shouted, "What do you want?" The crowd roared, "Black Power." Again, and again Ricks cried, "What do you want?" And the response "Black Power" grew louder and louder, until it had reached fever pitch. This moment was the birth of the Black Power slogan within the Civil Rights Movement.[18]

King knew Carmichael was becoming more militant, but he was surprised and disappointed that the phrase Black Power had been used at the rally. What he didn't understand is that Black Power was more than a slogan; it was a nascent movement that was destined to overshadow the Civil Rights Movement. King described a meeting he had with Carmichael and others to discuss their philosophical differences:

> It was my contention that a leader has to be concerned about the problem of semantics . . . While the concept of legitimate Black Power might be tentatively sound, the slogan "Black Power" carried the wrong connotations. I mentioned the implications of violence that the press had already attached to the phrase . . . Stokely replied that the question of violence versus nonviolence was irrelevant. The real question was the need for black people to consolidate their political and economic resources to achieve power.[19]

After the passage of the Civil Rights Act of 1964 and the Voting Rights Act of 1965, many young Blacks, like Carmichael, were disillusioned with the Civil Rights Movement. For some, the Movement promised much, but delivered little. Jim Crow was no longer a threat in the South, but in the North many Blacks lived in abject poverty, languishing in ghettos established by the federal government. Violence was rampant, dreams lay dormant, and opportunities were few.

In the mid-to-late 1960s, discontent erupted into uprisings in cities across the country. A now defunct publication, *Ramparts Magazine*, characterized the tumult in 1966, "After more than a decade of the Civil Rights Movement the black American in Harlem, Haynesville, Baltimore, and Bogalusa is worse off today than he was ten years ago . . . The Movement is in despair because it has been forced to recognize the Negro revolution as a myth."[20] If the Civil Rights Movement preached nonviolence and "Negro-white" unity, then the Black Power Movement championed self-defense and self-determination.

Henry Hampton's quiet demeanor and gentle voice belied a sharp intelligence and quick wit. His is not a household name, yet his impact on the Civil Rights Movement is immeasurable. Due to the convergence of "the black power movement and [his] own personal need for independence,"[21] Hampton created the production company Blackside, Inc. Twenty years later in 1987, *Eyes on the Prize*, his critically acclaimed documentary on the Civil Rights Movement, aired on PBS. Through the course of production, Hampton interviewed hundreds of people, which has served to document Black history for posterity.

In an interview with Hampton's production team on November 7, 1988, Carmichael revealed the impetus behind his doctrinal shift and that of SNCC. It began with a philosophical debate at Howard University in 1962 between Malcom X and longtime Civil Rights activist Bayard Rustin:

Bayard Rustin's approach was one of total commitment to nonviolence as philosophy with the aim of integrating into

the American capitalist system . . . Malcolm of course was
the total opposite, not seeing nonviolence as a philosophy,
almost denouncing it as a tactic . . . calling for violent clash
of arms against the American capitalist system and not for
integration . . . but separation from it, while seeking its
destruction . . . So, the Malcolm X debate and the Bayard
Rustin debate had a profound effect upon the nonviolent
action group and consequently SNCC . . . He gave us all
the intellectual arguments and opened up the way for us to
show clearly an intellectual basis for a nationalism and an
ability to smash all ideas that were in contradiction to it.
Malcolm opened up the way . . . for violence as a legitimate
weapon in a struggle for human rights.[22]

After the debate at Howard University, Malcolm X's ideology "began to take firm root inside of SNCC,"[23] culminating in
Carmichael's Black Power moment at the Meredith Mississippi
Freedom March four years later. Through the teachings of
Malcolm X and a belief that King's approach was no longer
effective, Carmichael concluded that Black people could only
achieve power if they closed ranks.

Carmichael imagined a Black-only community where
schools, organizations, banks, businesses, and more were Black-
owned and Black-lead—wholly independent from the "racist
institutions and values" of white society. Like Malcolm X, and
the Black Panther Party that followed, the Black Power credo
rejected integration:

Integration as a goal today speaks to the problem of blackness not only in an unrealistic way but also in a despicable
way. It is based on complete acceptance of the fact that in
order to have a decent house or education, black people

must move into a white neighborhood or send their children to a white school. This reinforces, among both black
and white, the idea that "white" is automatically supe-
rior and "black" is by definition inferior. For this reason,
"integration" is a subterfuge for the maintenance of white
supremacy.[24]

King's approach to integration was pragmatic. He believed it
was the only way Blacks could be free, "In our kind of society
liberation cannot come without integration and integration
cannot come without liberation . . . I cannot see how the Negro
will be totally liberated from the crushing weight of poor education, squalid housing, and economic strangulation until he is
integrated, with power, into every level of American life."[25] King
and Carmichael were locked in an ideological battle that did not,
visibly, and publicly, include Black women. Black men in leadership failed to seek the Black woman's opinion as they deliberated
the contours of power.

 While Black men, as explored in depth in chapter four, did
not have power in society at large—they dictated the terms of
power within the Black community. And too many Black women
(then and now) participated in their own erasure, surrendering
power for the redemption of Black men.

* * *

At a 1974 rally, Ella Baker strode swiftly and purposefully toward
the microphone stand at the edge of the stage. In her left hand she
tightly held her large black purse. Her right hand grabbed the mic.
At seventy-one, her voice rang clear and strong, "I have had about
forty or fifty years of struggle, ever since a little boy on the streets
of Norfolk called me a nigger. I struck him back. And then I had to

learn that hitting back with my fists one individual was not enough. It takes organization. It takes dedication. It takes the willingness to stand by and do what has to be done, when it has to be done."[26] Speaking for less than two minutes, Baker's words—which delineated how power creates change—electrified the crowd.

Less well-known than King or Rustin, Baker's impact on the Civil Rights Movement is equally important. Influence evident in her nickname: "Fundi," a Swahili word meaning a person who teaches a craft to the next generation.

In a speech a few years before the rally, Baker outlined what needed to be done in the "struggle for full dignity as a human being."[27] It required, she said, a "great deal of analytical thinking and evaluation of methods that have been used [and asking] where do we really want to go and how can we get there [?]"[28] A half century later, Fundi's lesson remains relevant—and I her pupil.

The methods used today were used in the past. Marches, speeches, rallies, demonstrations, and boycotts were successful in the mid-twentieth century, to the extent that Congress enacted new laws. But today, those same approaches are less successful. Consider that the John Lewis Voting Rights Advancement Act is stalled in the United States Senate. And though President Joseph R. Biden Jr. signed a police reform executive order on the second anniversary of Floyd's death, the George Floyd Justice in Policing Act is no closer to becoming the law of the land. Why are tried and true organizing tactics less effective? Is it because people are not protesting or voting? No. Black Lives Matter protests following Floyd's police murder resulted in the largest racial justice protests in decades, and the 2020 presidential election saw the largest number of voter turnout (particularly among Black and Brown folks) in US history. Organizing tactics are less impactful because existing power structures have learned how to quelch these methods of protest.

In 2016, San Francisco 49ers quarterback Colin Kaepernick kneeled as "The Star-Spangled Banner" played—protesting racism, police brutality, and the national anthem's pro-slavery lyrics. At the end of the season, Kaepernick became a free agent.

Although Kaepernick was unemployed and had ignited a cultural firestorm, the *New York Times* reported that Nike decided to keep him on their roster of sponsored athletes due to "the credibility the company would gain with the young, urban market it has long targeted."[29] Nike strategically sought to placate the Black community by retaining Kaepernick. If they had let Kaepernick go, they risked angering the Black community and faced potential boycotts.

Ironically, Nike did face boycotts—but from those who disagreed with Kaepernick's national anthem protest. They opposed Nike's decision to make the former quarterback central to its long-running "Just Do It" marketing campaign in 2018. CBS News reported that the gamble worked, as the sneaker behemoth's allegiance to the urban market (aka Black folks) paid off to the tune of billions of dollars:

> Nike shares have surged 36 percent on the year, making the company the top performer on the Dow's index of 30 blue-chip stocks. The run-up includes a nearly 5 percent increase since Nike's Labor Day announcement that Kaepernick would be featured in its campaign, adding nearly $6 billion to the company's market value.[30]

Nike's relationship with Kaepernick continues to be successful. To commemorate the fourth anniversary of Kaepernick kneeling, Nike released an all-black No. 7 jersey. Retailing at $150, the jersey sold out in under one minute. The inherent problem is that Nike gets to sell the idea that they are somehow advancing the cause of Black folks, but they are simply profiting from Black pain.

In 2020, the *Financial Times* reported on a group of Black Nike employees who raised "repeated objections to the release of a[n] ad . . . asking management to publicly acknowledge the company's own internal shortcomings on equality before promoting the ideal to consumers." The video featured elite Afro-descendant athletes—LeBron James, Eliud Kipchoge, Caster Semenya, Giannis Antetokounmpo, Serena Williams, and Colin Kaepernick—promoting Nike's image as an "advocate for change"[31] that is making the "world better."[32]

Nike's penchant for socially conscious marketing changes little except to make the already wealthy, even wealthier. In this way, corporate bureaucracy, rather than the government, mollified the masses, the legacy and meaning of Kaepernick's protest subsumed by flashy corporate videos. The appearance of corporate solidarity and allyship are a mirage.

Due to the large-scale protests in 2020, Nike and many other businesses released statements, social posts, and video ads in support of Black Lives Matter. Many of these statements accompanied empty promises to change hiring practices and to stand with Black people. But I question if those efforts produced meaningful, lasting improvements in the lives of Black folks.

A cycle repeats itself ad nauseam. It's what I call the power share illusion. First, there is a common need or lack experienced by a marginalized group. The subordinate group organizes into a movement. The purpose of this movement is to ask the dominant group for something—to share its resources, money, clout, privilege. In essence, the ask is to share power. If enough hell is raised, those in power "seemingly" capitulate. In truth, the powerful never relinquish real, lasting power.

5

66 POWER

* * *

The *Washington Post* headline from May 18, 1954, read, "Separate But Equal Doctrine is Thrown Out." The landmark *Brown vs. Board of Education* Supreme Court decision challenged not only segregation in schools but the very premise of Jim Crow laws. It signaled a seismic shift in US culture. That is, until it didn't.

In 1960, the neoconservative monthly magazine *Commentary* reported on the ineffectiveness of the *Brown* decision, "If school integration in the South were to continue at its 1959 rate, it would take four thousand years for all Southern Negro children to achieve their right to equal educational opportunity."[33] Four. Thousand. Years.

The failure of racial desegregation in public school didn't just happen. As explained by Dr. Martin Luther King Jr., beginning in 1955, states across the South enacted Pupil Placement laws to prevent Black children from matriculating to white schools:

> The placement laws are designed to perpetuate segregation by integrating the fewest possible number of Negro students . . . the states of Alabama, Arkansas, Florida, Louisiana, North Carolina, Tennessee, Texas, and Virginia, and the city of Atlanta, Georgia, have all adopted placement laws, and it appears that other states and cities will follow suit. The specific provisions and requirements of the placement laws vary widely from state to state, but the purpose is the same everywhere.[34]

Although these states were noncompliant, the constitutionality of the Pupil Placement laws were subsequently upheld by the US Supreme Court. As King noted, "in effect returning to the states the power to determine the tempo of change."[35] Seventy years later, success is murky. Black students in the twenty-first century graduate from high school at higher rates than our predecessors, yet the quality of that education is suspect and the percentage of public schools that are segregated along racial and economic lines not only stubbornly remains but continues to grow.

The aftermath of the Civil War provides yet another example of the power share illusion. The era of Reconstruction was a hopeful time for formerly enslaved people. Black people enrolled in school, opened businesses, purchased land, and Black men got the right to vote and hold political office.

In direct response to these gains, white people, particularly in the South, began to systematically terrorize Black people into submission. Intentional disciplinary methods were employed (Jim Crow laws, Black Codes, lynching, peonage, the Ku Klux Klan) to normalize a social construct centered on keeping Black folks enslaved. And for decades, their method worked.

Imagine a group of children playing with a ball. Another child, a neighbor perhaps, asks if they can play with the ball too. What are the chances that the children with the ball will give it to the child who doesn't have a ball? Let's suppose the same group of children allow their neighbor to join in the game, but soon after they unexpectedly change the rules and now, their neighbor rarely (if ever) gets to touch the ball. Under our existent systems of oppression, those in power do not give it away and they do not fully share it. Their inclination is to hold onto power.

True power is never requested but taken. Throughout history, power has primarily been taken by force: thirteen North American colonies waged war to gain independence from Britain; enslaved Africans in Haiti defeated three Western armies to establish the Republic of Haiti in 1804. There are numerous examples throughout history, but in the modern era, violence is not a viable option. Embracing violent tactics and a self-defense ethos did not work for the Black Power Movement, Black Panthers, nor the Nation of Islam. The allure of violence to secure equity is seductive, but each of those groups failed to establish a viable military force.

There's been incremental change over the years, but many Black people have felt that they were always, somehow, left holding the bag. Affirmative Action was meant to level the playing field; instead it left Black folks vulnerable to self-doubt and accusations that they did not deserve what they had earned.

Ella Baker argued that in order for "poor and oppressed people to become a part of a society that is meaningful, the system under which we now exist has to be radically changed."[36] The focus has always been on what Black folks want. Not on what Black folks need to get what they want. It is not enough to desire fair housing, a livable wage, or an end to police brutality and misogynoir. These desires, as Bertrand Russell argues, must be accompanied by a "love of power" if there is to be societal change.

I do not consider Russell's "love of power" a diabolical, Machiavellian love. Rather, it is an understanding that power is a tool. And the right tool is essential to getting the job done.

In order to cook, one needs to produce heat. Several hundred years ago, a pot over an open fire sufficed, but today a pot placed on an electric or gas stove is a much better tool for cooking.

Likewise, the "love of power" is the necessary tool to advance societal change. To use power, Black women need to identify what they want, formulate a strategy to get it, and then run after it with everything they have.

What do Black women want? This is a complex question. There are approximately twenty-four million Black women in this country. And they are not a monolith. There are Black women who can trace their ancestors back to a southern plantation. Others who have emigrated from the Caribbean or Africa. There are Black women who struggle to put food on the table. And some who have amassed wealth. There are liberals and conservatives, Marxists and capitalists, Christians, Muslims. Yet those differences don't preclude what they really want, what they've always wanted.

Baker describes an ideal society. It esteems the "dignified existence [of a] human being, that permits people to grow and develop according [to] their capacity, that gives them a sense of value, not only for themselves, but a sense of value for other human beings."[37] It is a society many could support, but to realize a society like the one Baker imagines requires an awareness and appropriate utilization of power.

* * *

The white man's exercise of power looks like neocolonialism, imperialism, white supremacy, patriarchy, and other dominating forms of oppression. However, wielding power like a Black woman differs greatly.

I am not claiming that all or even a few Black women exercise power in the way I am going to describe, but it is possible that there are Black women who employ similar methods or points of view and may not think of it as wielding power. It is a strategy I developed working for over two decades as a news producer and digital media executive in New York City. It has been effective because it has enabled me to achieve goals without compromising my value system.

Wielding power like a Black woman does not seek to oppress others on the way to getting what one wants. Neither does it replicate normative methods that uphold oppressions like white supremacy and patriarchy. To wield power like a Black woman is to identify a goal, dream, or desire and then work toward it with persistence, confidence, and patience. It relies on strategy, innovation, planning, and flexibility. It's about being honest, transparent, and never steamrolling over others.

At the beginning of this chapter, I shared a work experience. As I explained, it took time to achieve the goal of running the video team. I understood that no one was invested in that goal more than me, and I was aware that my colleague would be impacted by my promotion. Throughout the process in advocating for myself, I did not malign my colleague, make up stories, or cause dissension. I was forthright and honest in conversations with my boss and other senior leaders. After the team's reorganization, I continued to treat my colleague with respect. For nearly three years, we had a wonderful working relationship, and throughout that time I truly valued his support, knowledge, and contributions.

In the preface to the revised tenth anniversary edition of *Black Feminist Thought*, Collins wrote how her ideas of empowerment evolved from the book's 1990 edition:

> I now recognize that empowerment for African American women will never occur in a context characterized by oppression and social injustice. A group can gain power in such situations by dominating others, but this is not the type of empowerment that I found within Black women's thinking . . . Black feminist thought works on behalf of Black women but does so in conjunction with other similar justice projects.[38]

What Collins came to understand is that Black women have no interest in oppressing others to get what they want. Collins's observation highlights a potential reason many Black women are reluctant to exercise power in a way that will create lasting societal change. It is logical that power, framed in the image of white men, is distasteful to Black women. The thirst for power, domination, and wealth has wreaked global pain, chaos, and death. But Black women must be willing to wield power. Not like how a white man exercises power, but through collaboration, partnership, and defined outcomes that are mutually beneficial.

Collins outlines two approaches to exercising power: dialectical and subjectivity. The dialectical approach "emphasize[s] the significance of knowledge in developing self-defined, group-based standpoints that, in turn, can foster the type of group solidarity necessary for resisting oppressions."[39] In other words, forming solidarity that is based on group identity inspires actions that can lead to social change.

The subjectivity approach "emphasize[s] how domination and resistance shape and are shaped by individual agency."[40] Contrary to the dialectical approach, subjectivity focuses on the ways "self-definitions and behaviors shift in tandem with a changed consciousness concerning everyday lived experiences."[41] Meaning, how an individual engages and resists is determined by the varied oppressions encountered by that individual. And Black women, as detailed in chapters two and three, already possess the consciousness and the ingredients to the *secret sauce*, which acts as a deterrent to oppression. And as oppression is resisted on an individual basis, it forces power structures to weaken and change. Collins's dialectical and subjectivity approaches to exercising power and my assertion to wield power like a Black woman are ways that we can effectively employ power.

In 2020, the *New York Times* conducted an analysis of more than nine hundred officials and executives in prominent,

powerful positions across a host of public and private indus-
tries.[42] Their report found that though the US is more diverse
than ever, 80 percent of those in power are mostly white. This is
problematic.

I assert that Black women collectively work toward infil-
trating these power structures; it is where and how decisions
are made. While I concede that, in a pluralistic society, Black
women will need to work across divides, our strategy cannot be
one of dependence, waiting for others to show up on our behalf.
Allyship or waiting for someone to share power is not the same
as agency or being motivated by a love of power.

Shirley Chisholm did not wait for the leaders of the
Democratic Party to ask her to run for the presidential nomina-
tion in 1972. Wielding power, Chisholm ran a campaign with the
best slogan ever: "Unbought and Unbossed." At fifteen, Claudette
Colvin did not ask the leaders of the NAACP if she should refuse
to give up her seat to a white woman in Montgomery, Alabama.
Colvin was arrested at least eight months before Rosa Parks
refused to relinquish her seat.

At every instance, in every aspect, we should look for
opportunities to wield power. And then take that power and
change the life of every Black person for the better. If we do this
with intention, if we truly go after it, within a generation we will
have a very different nation.

Black women have power. That power is built on the connection, love, and trust that Black women share for one another.
As noted in an earlier chapter, the Marist Poll found that nearly
80 percent of Black women agree they are part of a sisterhood
and most Black women (83 percent) trust other Black women.
The power of Black women shows up in the census data, that
proves Black women over an eighty-year[43] span saw record rates
of growth in real median wages, completion of college, and in

professional/managerial jobs. Power is evident in the number of Black women whose votes have changed the outcome of elections. From the 2016 and 2020 presidential elections and the 2018 midterm elections, more than 90 percent of Black women voted along Democratic Party lines, arguably cementing them as the Democrat's most important voting bloc.

The question isn't about whether Black women have power; it is about whether Black women will accept that a "love of power" is needed to effectuate societal change. It is whether Black women are willing to recognize and collectively wield power.

As we move forward, let's operationalize a strategy of power based on Dr. Martin Luther King Jr.'s analysis.

Power and morality must go together, implementing, fulfilling, and ennobling each other . . . Power at its best is the right use of strength. The words of Alfred the Great are still true: "Power is never good unless he who has it is good." . . . It will be power infused with love and justice, that will change dark yesterdays into bright tomorrows, and lift us from the fatigue of despair to the buoyancy of hope.[44]

CHAPTER 8

DE NOVO (A NEW BEGINNING)

In Jewish and Christian religious texts, King Solomon is the wisest person to have ever lived. As the last sovereign of the ancient Kingdom of Israel, he authored the scroll of Kohelet (Ecclesiastes in English), which are writings that grappled with the meaning and futility of life. In the Kohelet, Solomon famously wrote "better is the end of a thing than the beginning thereof."[1] A sentiment true of Black women writ large and one foremother in particular.

Between 1820 and 1822, on the Eastern shore of Maryland in Dorchester County, Harriet Tubman was born enslaved. But nearly a century later she died a freed woman in Auburn, New York. Tubman's liberty did not wait for a presidential proclamation, neither did it depend on the Union prevailing over the Confederates. Faced with the possibility of being sold deeper into the South to a chain gang, Tubman embarked on a journey to free herself.

Hiding by day.

Walking by night.

Fortified by faith.

Tubman deemed freedom worth the arduous journey to Philadelphia and risk of capture. When the North Star guided her to the Mason-Dixon line in 1849, Tubman told her biographer, "I looked at my hands . . . to see if I was the same person now I was free. Dere was such a glory ober eberything, de sun came like gold trou de trees, and ober de fields, and I felt like I was in heaven."[2] After more than a quarter of a century enslaved, Tubman's escape north was the catalyst for her *de novo*—a brand-new beginning.

Unlike most of our foremothers, Tubman's story is well-known in the United States and around the world. Actress Cynthia Erivo was nominated for an Academy Award, Golden Globe, and Screen Actors Guild award for her portrayal of the abolitionist in the 2019 feature film *Harriet*. For nearly two centuries, Tubman's impressive resume as an Underground Railroad conductor, nurse, suffragist, and spy for the Union Army has inspired generations.

Born into a world that denied her the right to exercise free will, I've often marveled at Tubman's capacity to make hard, courageous choices. On that 1849 trek north, two of Tubman's brothers were with her, but early in the journey they turned back, afraid of being captured. Her hard, courageous choice? To continue on.

Tubman's newfound freedom meant an opportunity to make decisions about her life and future. Her hard, courageous choice? Jeopardize her own freedom to lead dozens, and by some accounts hundreds, out of bondage over the course of a decade.

Tubman can't be understood in the context of the twenty-first century Black woman. The idea that an African descendant woman, born into the barbaric US slavery economy, would choose again and again and again to put her freedom and life in peril is remarkable. Tubman is a Black woman who got free and then freed others.

* * *

I am free. And freeing other Black women is on my agenda. It is why I wrote this book.

My freedom is not physical. But it breaks very real chains by reframing narrative and perspective. It is reminding Black women of our innate dope*ness*. It is the Black woman's inner knowing of Black women, an idea I wrote about in chapter one. It is that knowing that enables Black women to reject stereotypes and myths proliferated in the media, academia, and in hearts and minds.

In many ways, Black women already embrace our dope*ness*, that's why we say things like "Black Girl Magic" or "Black Girls Rock." While these affirmations are based on an inner knowing, an inner truth we have about ourselves, they don't go deep enough to get at the truth of how we do the do. It is why those affirmations ring a little hollow, almost as if we're trying to convince ourselves.

I got free because my inner knowing of Black women is not based on catchphrases but rooted in data that confirms what I know to be true about Black women: we are dope. So, what does dope*ness* look like in data?

The data from the decennial census and the American Community Survey explored throughout the book analyzed Black women as a group. It was important to understand how we are doing, compared to ourselves over an extended period. The analysis of the data shows that in the last eighty years[3] (1940–2019) Black women ages twenty-five to sixty-four have seen high rates of growth in median real wages (1000 percent), the completion of four or more years of college (1900 percent), and employment in professional/managerial occupations (700 percent).

But the data revealed a few surprises. When Black women as a group were compared to Black men, white men, and white women, ages twenty-five to sixty-four over the same eighty-year span, Black women had the largest percentage of growth in nearly all of the aforementioned variables. The story told by the data is completely different than the stories usually told about Black women. This is the result of two things: first, white men (and white women) are centered as the rubric and gold standard by which all groups are measured; second, data analysis usually does not compare group performance over a long time span, using the variables examined in this book.

I will explain it another way. In traditional studies on income, occupation, and education, white men are always ahead of Black women. But by directly comparing Black women as a group and white men as a group for nearly a century, the story we tell ourselves about Black women and white men are suddenly unrecognizable.

In the first chapter, I used a popular Aesop Fable to illustrate how Black women have been oppressed by white supremacy and patriarchy for centuries. I explained that Black women were typified by the slow-moving Tortoise, who won the race in an upset. And society was epitomized by the Hare, considered the fastest forest creature, but due to arrogance and temerity suffered a humbling defeat. But this time let's substitute white men for the Hare in the fable and compare results.

When Black women and white men are compared side by side, the census data showed that the rate of growth for Black women far exceeds the rate of growth for white men in all of the variables examined. When considering real media wages (adjusted for inflation), the rate of growth for white men and Black women aged twenty-five to sixty-four from 1940–2019 was 300 percent and 1000 percent respectively.

When looking at the completion of four years or more of college, with the same age group, over the same period, white men's rate of growth increased 500 percent, while the rate of growth for Black women completing four years or more of college was 1900 percent.

And finally, when evaluating the rate of growth in employment in professional/managerial roles, using the same age group and time span, white men's rate of growth was 300 percent, while Black women's rate of growth in professional/managerial roles was 700 percent. It is worth noting, while white men's rate of growth in service (domestic) work *increased* 200 percent over eighty years, Black women's growth in service work was negative—that is, the proportion of Black women declined from 68 percent in 1940 to 26 percent in 2019. Today, Black women earn just .64 cents to every dollar a white man earns, but the data I presented shows that the gap is closing. Just as the Tortoise was confident in his ability to win the race, I am confident that Black women can win too. It is only a matter of time.

The data presented in this book reframes the narrative of Black women. It shifts the framing of the problems we need to solve. The question isn't, why hasn't there been more progress? It should be how can we amplify and support the successful work Black women have been doing for decades? How can we accelerate the rise that's already happening and close gaps more quickly? I posit that a framing that celebrates and centers Black women's agency and success would be transformational. The idea isn't to pretend there isn't much to do, but approach the work from a position of strength.

Results from the exclusive, national Marist Poll, presented for the first time here, revealed that nearly 90 percent of Black women agree that the successes of Black women are generally overlooked and ignored by society and nearly eight in ten (78 percent) feel that Black women have less opportunity in life than other groups in society. For nearly two centuries, Black women have been working to shine a light on our accomplishments and contributions to society. And yet, it is clear most of us don't believe society cares about Black women.

The Marist Poll also shows that 70 percent of Black women say they have been successful in life, nearly 20 percent say they have been very successful in life. Just 5 percent of Black women say they have not been successful.

As I consider these diverging results, I am reminded of Dr. Lorick-Wilmot's Triple Identity Consciousness theory and the resistance inherent within bell hooks's oppositional gaze. My freedom is predicated on leaning into what I know to be true about Black women, what I've learned from the data, and the fact that most Black women say they have been successful in life. I actually don't care if society gets Black women or not. And it's time for all Black women to decide if it matters if society, or white people or any other group, sees us. It is my view that Black women are at a point in this country that our ability to create a life of our choosing is possible. Is it easy? No. Is it fair? No. But is it possible? Yes.

Reframing the narrative is as much about having the right information as reframing perception is redefining the problem. For centuries, Black women in the United States have pushed to be seen, whether we did it within or outside the system, peacefully or militantly; we have been asking not to be ignored. I assert that Black women can operate transactionally and functionally in society, without needing its validation. How much should I care if the white person at the store finds value in my humanity, what I offer the world? Not much, as long as I am aware, wary, and treated with respect. What I really care about is transacting for goods and services and being able to fully engage in this world. What Black women must do is engage with and change society, not retreat from society.

Harriet Tubman is remarkable for another reason. Based on how and when she grew up, it should have been impossible for her to do what she did. To what extent do we as Black women today decide that we have amassed enough power to live in our truth? Resistance can be fought in the streets, but it can also be fought in how we think about ourselves and how we own the stories of our lives. Today, there are a lot of reasons Black women can look at the glass half empty but remember Tubman didn't own a glass. And still she never allowed the white folks she was forced to call master and mistress to "own" her; that is evident in her actions.

The Marist Poll asked Black women if they think it is the best time to be a Black woman in America, a good time, a bad time, or the worst time. A majority of Black women (55 percent) think it is a good time to be a Black woman in the United States.

When we asked respondents to explain why they felt that way, most of the reasons fell into three distinct groups. The outright optimistic group: "Black women have more opportunities than ever before" or "Black women are finally being recognized more in society." The cautiously optimistic group: "Things aren't great and it's always a struggle being a Black woman, but it's better than it's ever been" or "Discouragement is all around, and you can either keep pursuing what you want or give up." And lastly, the society is irrelevant group: "Anytime is a good time to be a Black woman" and "Black women remain Black women despite what point in history they're in. It's always a 'good time' to be who you are." Whether Black women felt it was the best, good, bad, or worst time to be a Black woman varied across age and income. Black women were all over the spectrum in terms of who was more likely to feel one way or the other and why they felt the way they did.

When I first had the idea to write this book seven years ago, my premise was that it was the best time in America to be a Black woman. And I still believe that, but our history has shown us that it behooves Black women to hold onto inner knowledge, passed on from our foremothers, who whisper "it is always a good time to be a Black woman."

We should hold on to our *secret sauce*—composed of knowledge from our foremothers, creativity, faith, and sisterhood. The *secret sauce* is the sweet ingredient in the Lemonade Lifestyle—a methodology for living with intention, agency, and audacity to overcome life's lemons by blending joy, love, and rest into our lives.

To take care of our wellbeing also means reframing our relationship with Black men, to reject patriarchy and demand full, equal footing. Most Black women (95 percent) believe that sex discrimination against Black women is a problem in the Black community, and it's time to do something about it.

Let's reframe our interactions with white women. While six in ten Black women (57 percent) say they trust white women, nearly four in ten Black women (43 percent) say they do not. Like many Black women, I have amazing one-on-one relationships with white women, but historically as a group, I do not trust them. There are a sizable number of Black women who also struggle with trusting white women.

I advocate for Black women throughout the Americas to join in unity, an important form of power. And because society is built on relationships to power, how Black women navigate power, understand our power, and how we choose to use it is vital.

* * *

I have returned to Alisha Gordon throughout the book, because her narrative serves as a microcosm of Black women in the United States.

Like the majority (56 percent) of the US Black population living in the South, Gordon lived more than thirty years in Georgia. During her childhood, three to four days out of the week were spent in a Black church. Not uncommon for Black families, and it certainly was my experience, as well. Gordon was a first-generation college student, similar to many Black women, and she had to navigate a post-secondary education on her own.

Gordon's unplanned pregnancy revealed how some Black women face harsher consequences for missteps in life. Like the 45 percent of Black women who will experience intimate partner violence in their lifetime, Gordon was verbally and physically abused during her pregnancy. And a Bachelor of Arts degree and employment as a high school English teacher did not guarantee a livable wage. Caring for a child on her own made welfare assistance necessary.

A friend of Gordon's aptly described her life as a series of quantum leaps—quitting her teaching job, writing the viral *Huffington Post* article, graduating from seminary, and the most recent leap: New York. For Gordon, it's been providential, "There are these moments where God has carried the thread all the way through and led me to the work that I'm doing now at the Current Project to help Black single mothers close the socioeconomic gap for themselves."[4] On July 29, 2016, Gordon boarded an airplane in Atlanta headed north to a freedom of her own making. And like Tubman, Gordon could have focused on creating a cushy life for herself and her daughter, but ultimately, she chose to leverage her own freedom to free others. Gordon is a Black woman who got free and then went to work liberating other Black single mothers.

Freedom is critically thinking about the methods Black women employed to do so much with so little. It's not happenstance that Black women rise.

The Marist Poll, in an open-ended question, asked Black women if they believe the success, power, and influence of Black women in the United States will rise or fall in the twenty-first century. While most believe Black women will rise, uncertainty is mixed with hope. Here are some of those responses:

"Rise. I think that Black women have always been a force, but often in-service to other people and in the coming century I hope we'll flex that power and increasing opportunity for our own needs and desires."

"It's inevitable that the success, power, and influence of Black women in the US will rise in the twenty-first century."

"My hope is yes. Black women are evolving and trying to help each other more. We still have a long way to go, but we are going in the right direction."

"It will rise. We are determined to make it happen. We are going to rise . . . slow and steady."

"I believe the power and success of Black women will rise. We're FINALLY taking our rightful place in this world."

"Rise, because we have the determination to make it happen. We are used to struggling and making sacrifices to get what we want."

"It will rise. There are too many successful Black women who are paving the way and achieving success in all areas."

"We will run this country."

EPILOGUE

A CALL TO TWENTY-FIRST-CENTURY BLACK WOMEN

Twenty-first-century Black women stand at a crossroad. You know who you are.

How we got here is an amalgam of choices, circumstances, histories, and predestinations. And now we stand at a fork in the road, and it is time for this generation of Black women to choose.

There are two paths. Both operate in the reality of Black women's lived experiences. It is a reality bell hooks called imperialist white supremacist capitalist patriarchy; Kimberlé Crenshaw, intersectionality; Isabel Wilkerson, caste; and Nikole Hannah-Jones, 1619.

One path sees the reality, subsumes the messages of said reality, and accepts reality as a *fait accompli*. The other path sees the same reality, yet critiques the messages of that reality, rejecting, as described by feminist Elizabeth Janeway, the powerful's definition of reality.

Generations of Black women have had to face this crossroad. It may seem counter-intuitive that we are predetermined to arrive at the same intersection as our foremothers. It may feel like we're going backward, losing ground, running out of steam, but for now it is reality.

My understanding of our reality is augmented by a hopeful truth. Strides toward liberation have been made; the path is exponentially easier because of our foremothers. And as a consequence, the data shows that Black women's rate of growth in real median wages, completion of four years or more of college, and in the number of professional roles is the biggest percentage increase of all the sex/race groups examined in this book. Forget the reality peddled by oppressors. Data is reality. And it is telling us that our reality is changing for the better.

And so, I say embrace the strategy of our foremothers. Hold onto the Black women's inner knowing of our worth and value—we are not who society says we are. You may feel or have experienced being overlooked, undervalued, underestimated, and ignored. But to live unbound is to recognize these experiences and feelings do not mirror the truth about you.

Approach each day determined to draw on the strengths of the Black women's *secret sauce*: our foremothers, our creativity, our faith practices, and our sisterhood. The community and solidarity found in *secret sauce* is our shield and sword—our defense and weapon.

Intentionally live the Lemonade Lifestyle. Like so many of our elders, take the bitterness of reality, add the sweetness of the *secret sauce*, and LIVE a life of joy and love. As my ninety-three-year-old grandmother likes to say, "Life is for the living!"

I understand that Black women are tired: of fighting, proving, existing in a world that does not value our lives or contributions. But remember our foremothers and what they survived for us.

Learn from past mistakes. Black women are strong (because we've had to be) but we're not superhuman. We must prioritize our health and wellbeing. We must embody the mantra of the Nap Ministry: "rest is resistance." We must move our bodies and eat whole foods daily. We must slow down enough to listen to our hearts, pay attention to our feelings, commune with our souls, and practice vulnerability and gratitude.

Liberation has taken far too long to realize, but like our elders, let's choose the path of resistance, not despair. Let's choose to keep rising. That is the true power of the Black woman.

ACKNOWLEDGMENTS

As a child, I found writing thank you notes laborious and tedious. But my mom insisted, persisted, and of course, prevailed.

Now as an adult, I am thankful I was schooled to be grateful, to show appreciation. Gratitude is best expressed early and often. Conveyance of thanks an act of humility, an act of grace, an act of love.

I will forever be grateful for the opportunity to write this book. The journey has taken unexpected twists and turns. Some wonderful, some not so wonderful. Through it all I have grown as a human, a daughter, a friend, and a sister.

First and foremost, I thank God. As the scriptures say, He rewards those who believe in Him and diligently seek Him. Those are and remain life-long goals.

I thank my family for their love and encouragement; my father (Donarell B. Elder), my mother (Alacia D. Kearse), my sister (Rebecca C. Elder), and my grandmother (Anna Jewel Barnette).

I thank my dear friend and sister Kristi Rodgers who encouraged me and walked alongside me every single step of the way. And a special recognition to my homegirl, Dr. Yndia

Lorick-Wilmot, this book could not have been written without her insight, knowledge, advice, and love.

Many thanks to my editor at Skyhorse Publishing, Caroline Russomanno, and my agent Joelle Delbourgo, your guidance and support have been essential.

And a special thanks to:

- Dr. Natasha Gordon-Chipembere, a dope Black woman who challenged me and held me down.
- Zainab Salbi, for connecting me to the right people and believing in me from the beginning.
- Caroline Pincus, the first person in the literary world to take a chance on me.
- Alex Wallace Creed, my one-time boss and forever mentor, who supported me in countless ways. I will forever be grateful to Alex and her husband Kenny (and their four-footed son Atticus) for hosting me for two weeks at their home for a much-needed Writer's Retreat.
- Lisa Weiss and Dr. Christine Tucker, long-time friends who somehow found the time to lend their talents, advice, and expertise.
- The team of family and friends who *read my book proposal and gave me feedback*!!: Sarah Harris, Danielle Rodgers, Zainab Salbi, Yolanda Robinson, James Rodgers, Jeanine Davis, Jeanie Anh, Katie Long, Krystin Martin, Dr. Christine Tucker, Claire Moncrief, Trinidad Arizmendi, Nilda Havrilla, Samuel Stephens, Kristi Rodgers, Lisa Weiss, Lorraine Kearse, and Dr. Yndia Lorick-Wilmot.
- Dr. Stephen Valocchi, my college thesis advisor and favorite professor, taught me everything I know

about sociology. (And a big thank you for picking up the phone twenty-plus years later!)
- Dr. Kathryn Sophia Belle and the La Belle Vie Writing Group for their support and encouragement.
- Barbara Carvalho, Stephanie Calvano, and Lee Miringoff at the Marist Poll for their early, continual, and tangible support.
- David Van Riper and Khoa Vu at the University of Minnesota, for providing and preparing US Census and the American Community Survey (ACS) data.
- Dr. Constance Citro, senior scholar at the Committee on National Statistics at the National Academies of Sciences, Engineering, and Medicine, for analyzing the data and creating awesome graphs.
- Jessica Suriano, for factchecking the manuscript and making sure that this book is as factually accurate as possible.

And last, but certainly not least, I thank all of the Black women, the descendants of enslaved Africans, who over the centuries and against the odds endeavored to tell the truth and bust myths about Black women. I share your burden; I stand on your shoulders, and I hope you're proud.

MARIST POLL OCTOBER 2021
SURVEY METHODOLOGY

This survey was conducted in two stages—a Random Digit Dialing (RDD) phone survey representative of the US national adult population and an online probability panel survey of Black Americans.

The RDD phone survey of 1,275 adults was conducted October 11 through October 13, 2021, by Marist Poll. Adults eighteen years of age and older residing in the contiguous United States were contacted on landline or mobile numbers and interviewed by telephone using live interviewers. Survey questions were available in English or Spanish. Mobile telephone numbers were randomly selected based upon a list of telephone exchanges from throughout the nation. The exchanges were selected to ensure that each region was represented in proportion to its population. Mobile phones were treated as individual devices. After validation of age, personal ownership, and non-business-use of the mobile phone, interviews were typically conducted with the person answering the phone. To increase coverage, this mobile sample was supplemented by respondents reached through random dialing of landline phone numbers. Within each landline household, a single respondent was selected through a random selection process to increase the representativeness of traditionally under-covered survey populations. The samples were then combined and balanced to reflect the 2019 American Community Survey one-year estimates for age, gender, income, race, and region.

In order to analyze the opinions of Black Americans, online interviews with a representative oversample of 886 Black Americans were conducted using NORC's AmeriSpeak probability panel from October 4 through October 18, 2021. The survey questions were formatted for self-administration and optimized for mobile devices.

Both phone and online datasets were combined for a total of 2,161 Americans, including 966 Black Americans and 619 Black women. The resulting data were adjusted to reflect the overall adult population of Americans nationally. The results for adults overall are statistically significant within ±3.6 percentage points. The results for Black Americans and Black women are statistically significant within ±5.4 percentage points and ±6.7 percentage points, respectively.

Banners included results for subgroups to only display crosstabs with an acceptable sampling error. It should be noted that although you may not see results listed for a certain group, it does not mean interviews were not completed with those individuals. It simply means the sample size was too small to report. The error margin was adjusted for sample weights and increases for cross-tabulations.

US CENSUS AND AMERICAN COMMUNITY SURVEY

NOTES ON DATA

The data used for the analysis in this book come from the decennial census for the years 1940 through 2000. For 2010 and 2019, the data source is the American Community Survey (ACS), which included questions on occupation, income, and other characteristics that were previously included in the census for a sample of the population. The ACS for 2019 was used because the COVID pandemic adversely affected the response to the ACS in 2020.

The census and ACS Public Use Microdata Sample (PUMS) files that provided the data in the book are those maintained at the University of Minnesota by IPUMS USA. Gratitude is due to David Van Riper and Khoa Vue for producing the tables and to Dr. Constance Citro for analyzing the trends in the tables.

In order to make information on educational levels, occupations, and median annual wages more comparable across the eighty-year time span of the analysis, all of the variables were tabulated for people ages twenty-five to sixty-four. This age range is often referred to as working-age or prime-age adults, most of whom have completed their education and are not yet retired. Notes for each variable follow.

RACE

The analysis pertains to Black women and men and White women and men. For the 2000 census and 2010 and 2019 ACS, which allowed people to mark more than race, the categories are "Black alone" and "White alone."

EDUCATIONAL ATTAINMENT

Two variables were tabulated for people ages twenty-five to sixty-four: attainment of at least one year of college and attainment of at least four years of college.

OCCUPATION

The occupation categories are based on occupation reported for a person's job last week or, if not employed last week, for the most recent job. The categories use the OCC1950 variable from IPUMS USA to be able to include data for 1940. This variable standardizes occupational codes for all years to the Census Bureau's 1950 occupational coding scheme. The five categories in the analysis each sum two–three categories provided by IPUMS for people ages twenty-five to sixty-four:

- Laborers (farm and nonfarm)
- Service workers (private household and other)
- Crafts workers and operatives
- Clerical and sales workers
- Professional and technical workers and managers

The five occupational categories do not sum to 100 percent. They exclude farmers for all years. For the 1940–1960 censuses, they also exclude people who have a missing or unknown occupation because the Census Bureau did not impute or assign values for missing occupations in those years.

MEDIAN ANNUAL REAL WAGES (INFLATION-ADJUSTED)
The wage variable is median annual (gross) wages for people ages twenty-five to sixty-four in the labor force before taxes or any other deductions. The median is the middle value or the value that separates the population in half. It is a more informative and stable measure for variables like wages than the arithmetic mean or average, which can be pulled upward by people who make exceptionally high wages. The amounts for each decade are adjusted for inflation, using the Consumer Price Index (CPI) values from the Minneapolis Federal Reserve Bank (https://www.minneapolisfed.org/about-us/monetary-policy/inflation-calculator/consumer-price-index-1913-).

LABOR FORCE
People in the labor force include those at work last week and those not working but who are seeking work. About 79 percent of all Black and white prime-age adults were in the labor force in 2019.

QUALITY OF THE DATA
Data from the decennial census and the ACS are of high quality. This does not mean that they are without error, but errors are small (for more information, visit: Census.gov). Types of errors that could potentially affect the analysis in this book, but not likely to any significant degree, include:

- Sampling error—beginning with the 1950 census, the socioeconomic variables in the analysis were collected from large samples of the population rather than the entire population. (Everyone in the census answered a small set of questions, including age, sex, and race.) In addition, the tabulations prepared by IPUMS USA come from PUMS files, which are subsamples of the census or ACS samples. Sampling error or variability is very small, however, because the sample sizes are very large—the PUMS files include deidentified records for one in a hundred of the total population. This sampling fraction means that the 2019 ACS PUMS file included about three million person records.

- Failure to respond—not everyone provides an interview even after extensive follow-up. For example, 2 percent of the population were "whole-person imputations" in the 2000 census. The Census Bureau "imputes" or fills in the information for people who did not respond using information from other household members or from the neighborhood.

- Failure to answer all of the questions—most people (98 percent or higher in the 2019 ACS, for example) answer basic questions on age, sex, and race. Fewer people provide answers for socioeconomic questions. In the 2019 ACS, the Census Bureau had to impute or assign values for missing responses for educational attainment and labor-force status for about 10 percent of people, rising to 15 percent for occupation and 21 percent for annual wages. For censuses processed before full computerization, the Census Bureau published the numbers of people who failed to answer a question; for more recent censuses and the ACS, the Census Bureau uses computer routines to impute or fill in responses for every question.

- Inconsistencies across time—each census is conducted somewhat differently from the previous census, and the ACS collection methods differ in important ways from the census. Moreover, questions that appear to be the same over time may differ somewhat. For example, beginning with the 2000 census, respondents could check more than one race. To maximize comparability with earlier censuses, this analysis uses "White alone" and "Black alone" beginning in 2020.

Notwithstanding the potential quality concerns listed above, for an analysis of socioeconomic time trends by race and sex extending back to 1940, there is no substitute for the census and ACS.

NOTES

PREFACE

1. Scripture quotations taken from the Amplified® Bible (AMP), Copyright © 2015 by the Lockman Foundation. Used by permission; www.lockman .org.

CHAPTER 1: ACTS OF RESISTANCE

1. Paula Giddings, *When and Where I Enter: The Impact of Black Women on Race and Sex in America* (New York: William Morrow & Company Inc., 1984), 46.
2. The data used for the analysis is seventy-nine years, but for the purposes of readability we use eighty years. The data comes from the decennial census for the years 1940 through 2000. For 2010 and 2019, the data source is the American Community Survey (ACS), which included questions on occupation, income, and other characteristics that were previously included in the census for a sample of the population. The ACS for 2019 was used because the COVID pandemic adversely affected the response to the ACS in 2020.
3. George Yancy, "bell hooks: Buddhism, the Beats and Loving Blackness," *New York Times*, December 10, 2015, https://archive.nytimes.com/opinionator .blogs.nytimes.com/2015/12/10/bell-hooks-buddhism-the-beats -and-loving-blackness/.
4. Ibid.
5. Elizabeth Higginbotham, "Reframing work for black women: Master narratives as constraints to scholarship," filmed March 2009 at Rutgers University, New Brunswick, NJ, video, 5:26, https://www.youtube.com /watch?v=q9JHp0Y1kJM&t=728s.
6. "Mossell, Gertrude Bustill 1855–1948," Encyclopedia.com, April 25, 2022,

201

https://www.encyclopedia.com/education/news-wires-white-papers-and-books/mossell-gertrude-bustill-1855-1948.

7. Henry Louis Gates Jr., Gene Andrew Jarrett, ed., *The New Negro: Readings on Race, Representation, and African American Culture*, 1892–1938 (Princeton, NJ: Princeton University Press, 2021), 290.

8. Ibid, 296.

9. Pero Gaglo Dagbovie, "New Directions in African American Women's History," *The Journal of African American History*, Vol. 89, No. 3, (Summer, 2004): 241–261.

10. Elizabeth Higginbotham, "Reframing work for black women: Master narratives as constraints to scholarship," 6:46.

11. Henry Louis Gates Jr., Gene Andrew Jarrett, ed., *The New Negro: Readings on Race, Representation, and African American Culture, 1892–1938*.

12. Ibid, 296.

13. The data used for the analysis in this book come from the decennial census for the years 1940 through 2000. For 2010 and 2019, the data source is the American Community Survey (ACS), which included questions on occupation, income, and other characteristics that were previously included in the census for a sample of the population. The ACS for 2019 was used because the COVID pandemic adversely affected the response to the ACS in 2020.

14. Alisha Gordon, interview by author, New York, March 25, 2022.

15. Ibid.

16. Ibid.

17. Ibid.

18. Ibid.

19. "Important welfare statistics for 2022 REVIEWED," Lexington Law, March 14, 2022, https://www.lexingtonlaw.com/blog/finance/welfare-statistics.html.

20. Gordon, interview.

21. Ibid.

22. Ibid.

23. Ibid.

24. Thomas Wedell-Wedellsborg, "Are You Solving the Right Problems?," Harvard Business Review Magazine, (January–February 2017): 76–83.

25. Thomas Wedell-Wedellsborg, *What's Your Problem? To Solve Your Toughest Problems, Change the Problems You Solve* (Boston: Harvard Business Review Press, 2020), Chapter 1.

26. Gordon, interview.

27. Ibid.

28. W. E. B. Du Bois, *The Souls of Black Folk* (New York: A.C. McClurg & Co., 1903), (Reprint Digireads.com, 2019), 6.

29. Dr. Yndia S. Lorick-Wilmot, interview by author, Zoom, January 27, 2022.

30. Gordon, interview.

31. Anita Tai, "Mary J. Blige Opens Up On Learning To Celebrate Her Successes: 'It's Peace Of Mind,'" ET Canada, February 18, 2022, https://etcanada.com/news/869225/mary-j-blige-opens-up-on-learning-to -celebrate-her-successes-its-peace-of-mind/.

32. Ashley Crossman, "Power Definitions and Examples in Sociology," ThoughtCo, October 25, 2019, https://www.thoughtco.com/power-p2 -3026460.

33. Cheryl L. Woods-Giscombé, "Superwoman schema: African American women's views on stress, strength, and health," *Qualitative Health Research*, 20(5), (May 2010): 668–683.

34. Victoria Uwumarogie, "Broken Heart Syndrome Is On The Rise And The Superwoman Phenomenon Is Partly To Blame," *Essence Magazine*, February 22, 2022, https://www.essence.com/health-and-wellness/broken -heart-syndrome/.

35. Tori DeAngelis, "The legacy of trauma," *Monitor on Psychology*, 50(2). (February 2019), https://www.apa.org/monitor/2019/02/legacy-trauma.

CHAPTER 2: SECRET SAUCE

1. "How I Got Over" featuring Mahalia Jackson, music and lyrics by Clara Ward.

2. J'na Jefferson, "How Mahalia Jackson's legacy lives on through Gospel music and the fight for Civil Rights," the *Philadelphia Sunday*, April 2, 2021, https://www.philasun.com/entertainment/how-mahalia-jacksons -legacy-lives-on-through-gospel-music-and-the-fight-for-civil-rights/.

3. Ibid.

4. "How I Got Over" featuring Mahalia Jackson, music and lyrics by Clara Ward.

5. Ibid.

6. Ibid.

7. Willa Ward-Royster and Toni Rose, *How I Got Over: Clara Ward and the World-Famous Ward Sister* (Philadelphia: Temple University Press, 1997), 102–104.

8. Ibid.

9. Ibid.

10. Ibid.

11. Ibid.

12. Ibid.

13. Anna Jewel Barnette, interview by author, Athens, Georgia, July 26, 2020.

14. Ibid.

15. Ibid.

16. Kara Manke, "Does being a 'superwoman' protect African American women's health?," *Berkeley News*, September 30, 2019, https://news.berkeley .edu/2019/09/30/does-being-a-superwoman-protect-african-american -womens-health/.

17. Tricia Hersey, About section on personal website, last accessed on January 31, 2022, http://www.triciahersey.com/about.html.

18. Tempestt Hazel, "Tricia Hersey, a testimony on liberation theology and rest as inheritance," *Sixty Inches From Center*, October 8, 2020, https://sixtyinchesfromcenter.org/tricia-hersey-a-testimony-on-liberation-theology-and-rest-as-inheritance/.

19. The Nap Ministry (@TheNapMinistry), "Y'all think this is just about naps and in every article, podcast or meme I say this clearly and speak about it being deeply political work that is disrupting toxic systems . . .," Twitter, Dec 31, 2021, https://twitter.com/TheNapMinistry/status/1477125090777219073.

20. Alisha Gordon, interview by author, New York, March 25, 2022.

21. Alice Walker, *In Search of Our Mother's Gardens* (New York: Harcourt Inc., 1983), 234.

22. Ibid., 239.

23. Ibid., 238.

24. Ibid., 241.

25. Ibid., 242.

26. Ibid.

27. Susie Mitchell (name changed to protect identity), interview by author, December 26, 2021.

28. Ibid.

29. Ibid.

30. Ibid.

31. Ibid.

32. Ibid.

33. Ibid.

34. "Obits from the Athens Daily News," October 20, 1996, http://files.usgwarchives.net/ga/clarke/obits/athensdailynews/1996/20oct96.txt.

35. Ibid.

36. Jeff Diamant, "Three-quarters of Black Americans believe in God of the Bible or other holy scripture," Pew Research Center, March 24, 2021, https://www.pewresearch.org/fact-tank/2021/03/24/three-quarters-of-black-americans-believe-in-god-of-the-bible-or-other-holy-scripture/.

37. The Nielsen Company, "African-American Women: Our Science, Her Magic, African American Diverse Intelligence Report," 2017, https://www.nielsen.com/wp-content/uploads/sites/3/2019/04/nielsen-african-american-diverse-intelligence-report-2017.pdf.

38. Theola Labbé-DeBose, "Black women are among country's most religious groups," *Washington Post*, July 6, 2012, https://www.washingtonpost.com/local/black-women-are-among-countrys-most-religious-groups/2012/07/06/gJQA0BksSW_story.html.

39. Yvonne Chireau, "Black Magic Matters: Hoodoo as Ancestral Religion," filmed November 10, 2021 at Harvard University, Cambridge, Massachusetts, video, 14:49, https://cswr.hds.harvard.edu/news/magic-matters/2021/11/10.

40. Nylah Burton, "How some Black Americans are finding solace in African spirituality," *Vox*, July 31, 2020, https://www.vox.com/2020/7/31/21346686/orisha-yoruba-african-spirituality-covid.
41. Candice Marie Benbow, *Red Lip Theology: For Church Girls Who've Considered Tithing to the Beauty Supply Store When Sunday Morning Isn't Enough* (New York: Convergent Books, 2022), 156.
42. Ibid.
43. Diretha Franklin, interview by author, Zoom, June 11, 2020.
44. Laura Green, interview by author, Zoom, June 11, 2020.
45. Diretha Franklin, interview by author, Zoom, June 11, 2020.
46. Laura Green, interview by author, Zoom, June 11, 2020.
47. Ibid.
48. Angela Brady, interview by author, Zoom, June 11, 2020.
49. Diretha Franklin, Ruth Grayer, Laura Green, interview by author, Zoom, June 11, 2020.
50. Lena Wright Myers, *Black Women: Do They Cope Better?* (Englewood Cliffs, N.J: Prentice Hall, 1980).
51. Ibid.
52. Ibid.

CHAPTER 3: LEMONADE LIFESTYLE

1. Jesse J. Holland, "Researchers seek fuller picture of first Africans in America," *Associated Press*, February 7, 2019, https://apnews.com/article/north-america-us-news-race-and-ethnicity-africa-va-state-wire-3501ba52dba0455597b3e7a330d2f50c.
2. Ibid.
3. Nichelle Smith, "She was captured, enslaved and she survived. Meet Angela, the first named African woman in Jamestown," *USA Today*, December 16, 2019, https://www.usatoday.com/in-depth/news/nation/2019/10/16/slaverys-history-angela-first-recorded-african-woman-jamestown/3895860002/.
4. "The First Africans: Angela," Historic Jamestowne, accessed January 22, 2022, https://historicjamestowne.org/history/the-first-africans/angela/.
5. Brooke Bobb, "Here's the Actual Recipe for Beyoncé's Lemonade," Vogue, April 25, 2016, https://www.vogue.com/article/food-beyonce-lemonade-recipe.
6. Beyoncé Lemonade Album, Track #10 Freedom, 2016.
7. Ibid.
8. Dr. Kinitra D. Brooks, "Black Women, Beyoncé & Popular Culture" UTSA 'Lemonade' Class Syllabus, 2016. https://www.scribd.com/document/325661048/UTSA-Lemonade-class-syllabus.
9. Maiysha Kai, "The Bitter, the Sweet, and the Book: Beyoncé's Seminal Work Enters the Literary Canon with *The Lemonade Reader*," *The Root*, June 11, 2019, https://www.theroot.com/the-bitter-the-sweet-and-the-book-beyonces-seminal-w-1835382108.

10. Dr. Kinitra Brooks, interview by author, Zoom, Jan. 19, 2022.
11. Kaitlyn Greenidge, "Beyoncé's Evolution," *Harper's BAZAAR*, August 10, 2021, https://www.harpersbazaar.com/culture/features/a37039502/beyonce-evolution-interview-2021/.
12. Beyoncé Lemonade Album, Track #10 Freedom, 2016.
13. Ibid.
14. Sandra Hanson and John White, ed., *The American Dream in the 21st Century* (Philadelphia: Temple University Press, 2011), 3.
15. Ibid, 7.
16. Ibid, 3.
17. James Truslow Adams and Howard Schneiderman, *The Epic of America* (New York: Routledge, 2017), 404.
18. Sarah Churchwell, *Behold, America: The Entangled History of "America First" and "The American Dream"* (New York: Basic Books, 2018), 3.
19. Samantha Smith, "Most think the 'American dream' is within reach for them," Pew Research Center, October 31, 2017, https://www.pewresearch.org/fact-tank/2017/10/31/most-think-the-american-dream-is-within-reach-for-them/.
20. John Locke, 1689, Second Treatise of Government.
21. Samantha Smith, "Most think the 'American dream' is within reach for them," Pew Research Center.
22. Jamie Ballard, "In 2020, do people see the American Dream as attainable?," YouGov America, July 18, 2020, https://today.yougov.com/topics/politics/articles-reports/2020/07/18/american-dream-attainable-poll-survey-data.
23. Maya Angelou, *And Still I Rise: A Book of Poems* (New York: Random House, 1978).
24. Barack Obama, *The Audacity of Hope: Thoughts on reclaiming the American Dream* (New York: Crown Publishers, 2006), 356.
25. The data used for the analysis in this book come from the decennial census for the years 1940 through 2000. For 2010 and 2019, the data source is the American Community Survey (ACS), which included questions on occupation, income, and other characteristics that were previously included in the census for a sample of the population. The ACS for 2019 was used because the COVID pandemic adversely affected the response to the ACS in 2020.
26. Donna Kelley, Mahdi Majbouri, and Angela Randolph, "Black Women Are More Likely to Start a Business than White Men," *Harvard Business Review*, May 11, 2021, https://hbr.org/2021/05/black-women-are-more-likely-to-start-a-business-than-white-men.
27. Ibid.
28. Ibid.
29. Ibid.
30. Ibid.
31. Sophia Kunthara, "Black Women Still Receive Just A Tiny Fraction Of VC

Funding Despite 5-Year High," *Crunchbase*, July 16, 2021, https://news.crunchbase.com/news/something-ventured-black-women-founders/.

32. Ibid.
33. ProjectDiane: The State of Latina & Black Female Founders, Digitalundivided, 2020, https://www.projectdiane.com/.
34. Kelley, Majbouri, and Randolph, "Black Women Are More Likely to Start a Business than White Men," *Harvard Business Review*.
35. Ibid.
36. Laura Huang and Sarah Mehta, "Arlan Hamilton and Backstage Capital," Harvard Business School, Case 419–029, October 2018, (Revised October 2019), https://www.hbs.edu/faculty/Pages/item.aspx?num=55047.
37. Ibid.
38. Since the fund was announced in 2018, there hasn't been updates. The following year Backstage Capital was criticized in some news reports for not making progress. In Hamilton's book, *It's About Damn Time: How to Turn Being Underestimated Into Your Greatest Advantage,* she addressed the criticism and denied that the fund fell through. My fact checker reached out to several people at Backstage Capital to get clarity but never got a response.
39. Arlan Hamilton (@Arlanwashere), "They're calling it a 'diversity fund.' I'm calling it an IT'S ABOUT DAMN TIME fund," Twitter, May 6, 2018.
40. Natasha Mascarenhas and Dominic-Madori Davis, "Backstage Capital cuts majority of staff after pausing net new investments," *TechCrunch*, June 26, 2022, https://techcrunch.com/2022/06/26/backstage-capital-cuts-majority-of-staff-after-pausing-net-new-investments/.
41. Arlan Hamilton, "An important Backstage update + finding peace for yourself as a non-negotiable," Your First Million, podcast, 4:47, https://open.spotify.com/episode/5hUiQN7zj7dZlL2IK8U6To?si=6c10ce7f461748a5&nd=1.
42. Ibid, 5:00.
43. Ibid, 14:39.
44. "5 Black Women Changing the Investment Landscape," Create & Cultivate, June 4, 2020, https://www.createcultivate.com/blog/black-female-investors/.
45. bell hooks, "Moving Beyond Pain," https://bellhooksbooks.com/moving-beyond-pain/.
46. Ibid.

CHAPTER 4: A HOUSE DIVIDED

1. Bill Whitaker, "Crisis in Chicago," CBS News, January 1, 2017, https://www.cbsnews.com/news/60-minutes-crisis-in-chicago-gun-violence/.
2. Ibid.
3. Ibid.
4. Ibid.
5. Ibid.

6. "Teen guilty in 2016 killing of woman outside Bronzeville Starbucks sentenced to 35 years," ABC 7 Chicago (WLS), June 20, 2019, https://abc7chicago.com/yvonne-nelson-shooting-arrest-chicago/5355020/.

7. Ralph Ellis and Vivian Kuo, "Dwyane Wade's cousin Nykea Aldridge killed; 2 brothers charged," CNN, August 28, 2016, https://www.cnn.com/2016/08/28/us/chicago-dwyane-wade-cousin-nykea-aldridge-killed/index.html.

8. Peter Nickeas, "2nd teen charged with first double homicide of 2016," Chicago Tribune, January 20, 2016, https://www.chicagotribune.com/news/breaking/ct-sakinah-reed-donta-parker-murder-charges-20160119-story.html.

9. Ray Sanchez, "Chicago officer who shot Rekia Boyd resigns," CNN, May 18, 2016, https://www.cnn.com/2016/05/18/us/rekia-boyd-shooting-officer-resigns/index.html.

10. Evan Osnos, "The Chicago Police, Race, and the Legacy of Bettie Jones," The New Yorker, April 20, 2016, https://www.newyorker.com/news/news-desk/the-chicago-police-race-and-the-legacy-of-bettie-jones.

11. Glenn Collins, "Patriarchy: Is It Invention Or Inevitable?" *New York Times*, April 28, 1986, https://www.nytimes.com/1986/04/28/style/patriarchy-is-it-invention-or-inevitable.html.

12. Gerda Lerner, "Women and History," interview by Jeffrey Mishlove. *A Thinking Allowed*, Excerpt of interview on YouTube, uploaded August 28, 2010, video, 5:47, https://www.youtube.com/watch?v=R_PJwMpAgtQ.

13. Glenn Collins, "Patriarchy: Is It Invention Or Inevitable?" *New York Times*.

14. "Till, Emmett Louis Biography, July 25, 1941 to August 28, 1955," The Martin Luther King, Jr. Research and Education Institute at Stanford University, (page accessed on May 16, 2022), https://kinginstitute.stanford.edu/encyclopedia/till-emmett-louis.

15. Alicia Garza, "The 100 Most Influential People Of 2020: Black Lives Matter Founders: Alicia Garza, Patrisse Cullors and Opal Tometi," interview by Sybrina Fulton. *Time Magazine*, September 22, 2020, video, 0:06, https://time.com/collection/100-most-influential-people-2020/5888228/black-lives-matter-founders/.

16. Larry Buchanan, Quoctrung Bui, and Jugal K. Patel, "Black Lives Matter May Be the Largest Movement in U.S. History," *New York Times*, July 3, 2020, https://www.nytimes.com/interactive/2020/07/03/us/george-floyd-protests-crowd-size.html.

17. Ruth Tam, "'When They Call You a Terrorist': A Black Lives Matter leader details the life that turned her into an activist," *Washington Post*, January 20, 2018, https://www.washingtonpost.com/news/post-nation/wp/2018/01/20/how-patrisse-khan-cullorss-life-experiences-prepared-her-for-a-career-of-advocacy/.

18. Julie Tate, Jennifer Jenkins and Steven Rich, "1,046 people have been shot and killed by police in the past year," *Washington Post*, (updated)

May 4, 2022, https://www.washingtonpost.com/graphics/investigations
/police-shootings-database/.

19. Akasha (Gloria T.) Hull, Patricia Bell Scott, and Barbara Smith, ed., *All the Women Are White, All the Blacks Are Men, But Some of Us Are Brave*, 2nd Edition (New York: The Feminist Press, 2015), 13–22.

20. bell hooks, "discussing the black female and modern day feminism with bell hooks," interview by Lynette Nylander, i-D.*Vice*, September 30, 2016, https://i-d.vice.com/en_uk/article/wjde5q/discussing-the-black-female -and-modern-day-feminism-with-bell-hooks.

21. Kimberle Crenshaw, "Demarginalizing the Intersection of Race and Sex: A Black Feminist Critique of Antidiscrimination Doctrine, Feminist Theory and Antiracist Politics," University of Chicago Legal Forum, Vol. 1989: Iss. 1, Article 8, http://chicagounbound.uchicago.edu/uclf /vol1989/iss1/8.

22. Ibid.

23. Frederick Douglass, "What The Black Man Wants," speech given at the Annual Meeting of the Massachusetts Anti-Slavery Society, Boston (1865), https://www.blackpast.org/african-american-history/1865-frederick -douglass-what-black-man-wants/.

24. Ibid.

25. Paula Giddings, *When and Where I Enter: The Impact of Black Women on Race and Sex in America* (New York: William Morrow & Company Inc., 1984), 65.

26. Ibid, 68.

27. Martin Luther King Jr., "'I've been to the mountaintop" (ABC News, full transcript of the speech). Delivered April 4, 1968, in Memphis, Tennessee, https://abcnews.go.com/Politics/martin-luther-kings-final-speech-ive -mountaintop-full/story?id=18872817.

28. Ibid.

29. Ibid.

30. Margalit Fox,"Izola Ware Curry, Who Stabbed King in 1958, Dies at 98," *New York Times*, March 21, 2015, https://www.nytimes.com/2015/03/22 /us/izola-ware-curry-who-stabbed-king-in-1958-dies-at-98.html.

31. Akasha (Gloria T.) Hull, Patricia Bell Scott, and Barbara Smith, ed., *All the Women Are White, All the Blacks Are Men, But Some of Us Are Brave*, 2nd Edition.

32. Septima Poinsette Clark and Blythe LeGette, *Echo in My Soul* (New York: E.P. Dutton and Co Inc., 1962), 82.

33. "Septima Clark meets with a group of African-American students," Southern California Library for Social Studies and Research, https: //umbrasearch.org/catalog/4165b4ec4bdf236a266ff0064a1e35636132 7ec3.

34. Septima Poinsette Clark, "Oral History Interview with Septima Poinsette Clark," interviewed by Jacquelyn Hall, Southern Oral History Program Collection in the Southern Oral History Program Collection (#4007),

Southern Historical Collection, Wilson Library, University of North Carolina at Chapel Hill. Interview G-0016, July 25, 1976, docsouth.unc.edu/sohp/G-0016/G-0016.html.

35. Ibid.

36. Ibid.

37. Daina Ramey Berry and Kali Nicole Gross, *A Black Women's History of the United States* (Boston: Beacon Press, 2020), 171.

38. Lisa Leslie, "Lisa Leslie reflects on the legacy of Kobe Bryant," interview by Gayle King, CBS News, February 4, 2020, video, 3:10, https://www.cbsnews.com/news/lisa-leslie-reflects-legacy-kobe-bryant/.

39. Matthew Impelli, "Snoop Dogg Criticizes Gayle King for Mentioning Kobe Bryant's Sexual Assault Charge in Interview: 'What Do You Gain From That?'" Newsweek, February 6, 2020, https://www.newsweek.com/snoop-dogg-criticizes-gayle-king-mentioning-kobe-bryants-sexual-assault-charge-interview-what-1486086.

40. Lebron James (@KingJames), "Protect @LisaLeslie at all cost! You're a real Superhero!! Sorry you had to through that s*%#!!! We are our own worse enemies! #Mamba4Life," Twitter, February 6, 2020.

41. Doha Madani, "Snoop Dogg apologizes to Gayle King for attack over Kobe Bryant sexual assault question," NBC News, February 12, 2020, https://www.nbcnews.com/pop-culture/pop-culture-news/snoop-dogg-apologizes-gayle-king-attack-over-kobe-bryant-sexual-n1136151.

42. Gayle King, "Oprah's 2020 Vision Tour Visionaries: Gayle King Interview," interview by Oprah Winfrey in Denver, Colorado, March 7, 2020, video, 39:59, https://www.youtube.com/watch?v=klSFIzM6Ar8.

43. Bill Cosby (@BillCosby), "It's so sad and disappointing that successful Black Women are being used to tarnish the image and legacy of successful Black Men, even in death," Twitter, February 6, 2020.

44. Janell Ross, "Two decades later, black and white Americans finally agree on O. J. Simpson's guilt," *Washington Post*, March 4, 2016, https://www.washingtonpost.com/news/the-fix/wp/2015/09/25/black-and-white-americans-can-now-agree-o-j-was-guilty/.

45. "When Men Murder Women: An Analysis of 2019 Homicide Data," Violence Policy Center, September 2021, https://www.vpc.org/studies/wmmw2021.pdf.

46. Ibid.

47. Ibid.

48. S.G. Smith, J. Chen, K.C. Basile, L.K. Gilbert, M.T. Merrick, N. Patel, M. Walling, A. Jain, "The National Intimate Partner and Sexual Violence Survey (NISVS). 2010–2012 State Report." Atlanta, GA: National Center for Injury Prevention and Control, Centers for Disease Control and Prevention. (2017) https://www.cdc.gov/violenceprevention/pdf/NISVS-StateReportBook.pdf.

49. Lois Beckett and Abené Clayton, "At least four Black women and girls were murdered per day in the US last year," *The Guardian*,

October 6, 2021, https://www.theguardian.com/us-news/2021/oct/06/black-women-girls-murder-rate-us.

50. Kiana Cox and Jeff Diamant, "Black men are less religious than black women, but more religious than white women and men," Pew Research Center, September 26, 2018, https://www.pewresearch.org/fact-tank/2018/09/26/black-men-are-less-religious-than-black-women-but-more-religious-than-white-women-and-men/.

51. Ibid.

52. Alisha Gordon, interview by author, New York, March 25, 2022.

53. Candice Marie Benbow, "I'm A Single Christian Woman And I Like Sex," Madamenoire, November 5, 2018, https://madamenoire.com/1046607/im-a-single-christian-woman-and-i-like-sex/.

54. Candice Marie Benbow, *Red Lip Theology: For Church Girls Who've Considered Tithing to the Beauty Supply Store When Sunday Morning Isn't Enough* (New York: Convergent Books, 2022).

55. Taffi Dollar, *Gender Roles* (College Park, Georgia: Creflo Dollar Ministries, 2017), 10.

56. Ibid, 11.

57. Ibid, 12.

CHAPTER 5: UNBRIDGED

1. Kim McLarin, *Womanish: A Grown Black Woman Speaks on Love and Life* (New York: Ig Publishing, 2019), 16–17.

2. Blaine G. Robbins, "What is Trust? A Multidisciplinary Review, Critique, and Synthesis," Sociology Compass (October 10, 2016): 972–986, https://doi.org/10.1111/soc4.12391.

3. Ibid.

4. Alisha Gordon, interview by author, New York, April 15, 2022.

5. Ibid.

6. Korey T Johnson (@korey4baltimore), Instagram video, May 17, 2020, https://www.instagram.com/tv/CASxOlsJSdu/.

7. Ibid.

8. Ibid.

9. Ibid.

10. @angela_bodley, "White women wanna preach feminism so bad but when it comes to black women they dgaf." Twitter.

11. @anastasianQveen, "I am a whole feminist but what I've noticed is, it's feminism til it deals with Black women," Twitter.

12. @KEvoLving, "It is always baffling to me when women don't understand the plight of other women. Smdh," Twitter.

13. Stephanie Jones-Rogers, *They Were Her Property: White Women as Slave Owners in the American South* (New Haven & London: Yale University Press, 2019), xvii.

14. Ibid, ix, xi-xii, xvii.

15. Letitia M. Burwell, *A Girl's Life in Virginia Before the War* (New York: Frederick A. Stokes Company Publishers, 1895) Electronic Edition (Chapel Hill: University of North Carolina at Chapel Hill, 1998), 2–3 https://docsouth.unc.edu/fpn/burwell/burwell.html.

16. Ibid.

17. Ibid.

18. Sheri Parks, "'A Strong Black Woman': A Good Or Bad Thing?" interview by Allison Keyes, *NPR Tell Me More*, March 25, 2010, audio, 3:17, https://www.npr.org/templates/story/story.php?storyId=1251729.

19. Letitia M. Burwell, *A Girl's Life in Virginia Before the War*.

20. Elizabeth Cady Stanton, Susan Brownell Anthony, Matilda Joslyn Gage, *History of Woman Suffrage V2 1861–1876* (New York: Fowler & Wells Publishers, 1882), 94–95.

21. Ida B. Wells, "Lynch Law In America," speech to a Chicago audience, January 1900, BLACKPAST, July 13, 2010, https://www.blackpast.org/african-american-history/1900-ida-b-wells-lynch-law-america/.

22. Toni Morrison, "What the Black Woman Thinks About Women's Lib," *New York Times*, August 22, 1971, https://www.nytimes.com/1971/08/22/archives/what-the-black-woman-thinks-about-womens-lib-the-black-woman-and.html.

23. Ibid.

24. At the time the direct quote was made, it was widely believed that 53 percent of white women voted for Donald Trump during the 2016 presidential election. The number came from Edison Research exit polling. In 2018, The Pew Research center, using "validated voters" from official voting records, stated that 47 percent of white women voted for Trump.

25. Tamika D. Mallory, "The Women's March on Washington: Digital Season," filmed July 2020 at Sydney Opera House, Sydney, Australia, video, 09:17, https://www.youtube.com/watch?v=ci0-eGxPoMU.

26. Ibid.

27. Daisha Riley, "Grandmother Who Organized Washington March 'Felt Women Needed to Stand Up,'" ABC News, January 17, 2017, https://abcnews.go.com/US/grandmother-organized-washington-march-felt-women-needed-stand/story?id=44814367.

28. Vanessa Wruble, LinkedIn page, https://www.linkedin.com/in/infinitevanessa/.

29. At the time the direct quote was made, it was widely believed that 53 percent of white women voted for Donald Trump during the 2016 presidential election. The number came from Edison Research exit polling. In 2018, The Pew Research center, using "validated voters" from official voting records, stated that 47 percent of white women voted for Trump.

30. Julia Felsenthal, "These Are the Women Organizing the Women's March on Washington," *Vogue*, January 10, 2017, https://www.vogue.com

/article/meet-the-women-of-the-womens-march-on-washington?utm
_source=VOGUE_REG_GATE.

31. Leah McSweeney and Jacob Siegel, "Is the Women's March Melting Down?" *Tablet*, December 10, 2018, https://www.tabletmag.com/sections /news/articles/is-the-womens-march-melting-down.

32. Ibid.

33. Ibid.

34. Ibid.

35. Isabel Wilkerson, *Caste: The Origins of Our Discontents* (New York: Random House, 2020), 17.

36. Ibid, 17–18.

37. Tamika D. Mallory, "The Women's March on Washington: Digital Season."

38. Julia Felsenthal, "These Are the Women Organizing the Women's March on Washington," *Vogue*.

39. Vanessa Wruble, Personal Website: https://www.vanessawruble.com /okayafrica.

40. Tamika D. Mallory, *State of Emergency: How We Win in the Country We Built* (New York: Black Privilege Publishing, Atria, 2021), 158–159.

41. Ibram X. Kendi, *How to Be an Antiracist* (New York: One Word, 2019), 13.

42. Glennon Doyle, *Untamed* (New York: The Dial Press, 2020), 219.

43. Ibid, 217.

CHAPTER 6: UBUNTU (I AM BECAUSE WE ARE)

1. Andrea Jaramillo, "Colombia's First Black Vice President Brings Green Focus," *Bloomberg*, June 20, 2022, https://www.bloomberg .com/news/articles/2022-06-20/colombia-s-first-black-vice-president -brings-major-climate-focus.

2. Julie Turkewitz, "Francia Márquez—a former housekeeper and activist—is Colombia's first Black vice president," *New York Times*, June 19, 2022, https://www.nytimes.com/2022/06/19/world/americas/francia-marquez -vice-president-colombia.html.

3. Michael Stott and Gideon Long, "Francia Márquez shakes up Colombian politics with bid for vice-presidency," *Financial Times*, April 26, 2022, https://www.ft.com/content/1d8a6209-615b-4a26-9a68-08e36432be89.

4. Francia Márquez, "I Am Because We Are": A conversation between Francia a Márquez Mina and Angela Davis," interview by Mamyrah Dougé-Prosper, University of California, Sep 7, 2021, video, 32:15, https://www.youtube.com/watch?v=qOLZaA509dI.

5. Nkem Ifejika, "What does ubuntu really mean?" *The Guardian*, September 28, 2006, https://www.theguardian.com/theguardian/2006/sep/29/ features11.g2#.

6. Ibid.

7. Desmond Tutu, "Archbishop Desmond Tutu on 'Dignity'," Amnesty International, October 21, 2010, https://www.amnestyusa.org/archbishop -desmond-tutu-on-dignity/#.

8. Audre Lorde, *Sister Outsider: Essays & Speeches of Audre Lorde* (Berkeley: Crossing Press, 1984), 110.

9. DeNeen L. Brown, "Slavery's bitter roots: In 1619, '20 And odd Negroes' arrived in Virginia," *Washington Post*, August 24, 2018, https://www.washingtonpost.com/news/retropolis/wp/2018/08/24 /slaverys-bitter-roots-in-1619-20-and-odd-negroes-arrived-in-virginia/.

10. The Trans-Atlantic Slave Trade Database. 2019. SlaveVoyages. https: //www.slavevoyages.org (accessed May 27, 2022).

11. Colin Palmer, "Defining and Studying the Modern African Diaspora," *Perspectives on History*, September 1, 1998, https://www.historians.org /publications-and-directories/perspectives-on-history/september-1998 /defining-and-studying-the-modern-african-diaspora.

12. Ibid.

13. George, Yancy, "bell hooks: Buddhism, the Beats and Loving Blackness," *New York Times*, December 10, 2015, https://opinionator.blogs.nytimes .com/2015/12/10/bell-hooks-buddhism-the-beats-and-loving -blackness/.

14. German Freire, Carolina Diaz-Bonilla, Steven Schwartz Orellana, Jorge Soler Lopez, Flavia Carbonari, "Afro-descendants in Latin America: Toward a Framework of Inclusion," World Bank, 2018, https: //openknowledge.worldbank.org/handle/10986/30201.

15. Colin Palmer, "Defining and Studying the Modern African Diaspora," *Perspectives on History*.

16. Art Harris, "Louisiana Court Sees No Shades of Gray In Woman's Request," *Washington Post*, May 21, 1983, https://www.washingtonpost.com/archive /politics/1983/05/21/louisiana-court-sees-no-shades-of-gray-in -womans-request/ddb0f1df-ba5d-4141-9aa0-6347e60ce52d/.

17. Marta Moreno Vega, Marinieves Alba, Yvette Modestin, ed., *Women Warriors of the Afro-Latina Diaspora* (Houston: Arte Publico Press. 2012), 30.

18. Ibid, 42.

19. Ibid, 42.

20. Ibid, 42.

21. Ibid, 40.

22. Henry Louis Gates, Jr., *Black in Latin America* (New York: New York University Press, 2011), 11.

23. Lorne Foster, Stella Park, Hugh McCague, Marcelle-Anne Fletcher, and Jackie Sikdar, "Black Canadian National Survey Interim Report 2021," Institute for Social Research, York University and Canadian Race Relations Foundation, https://blacknessincanada.ca/wp-content /uploads/2021/05/0_Black-Canadian-National-Survey-Interim-Report -2021.2.pdf.

24. Melissa Nakhavoly, "The history of Black Lives Matter Toronto and its momentous fight for change," *Toronto City News*, February 4, 2021, https://toronto.citynews.ca/2021/02/04/the-history-of-black-lives-matter-toronto/.
25. "Grit." Merriam-Webster.com Dictionary, Merriam-Webster, https://www.merriam-webster.com/dictionary/grit (accessed May 17, 2022).
26. Angela Duckworth FAQ, https://angeladuckworth.com/.
27. Julie Hawks, "Policing Black Lives: A New Book on State Violence in Canada," *Black Perspectives*, October 10, 2017, https://www.aaihs.org/policing-black-lives-a-new-book-on-state-violence-in-canada/#.
28. Ibid.
29. Nina Lakhani, "Fears growing for five indigenous Garifuna men abducted in Honduras," *The Guardian*, July 23, 2020, https://www.theguardian.com/global-development/2020/jul/23/garifuna-honduras-abducted-men-land-rights.
30. Miriam Miranda, "Without Our Land, We Cease To Be a People: Defending Indigenous Territory and Resources in Honduras," interview by Beverly Bell, Huffington Post, October, 26, 2013, https://www.huffpost.com/entry/-without-our-land-we-ceas_b_3816825.
31. "Marielle Franco murder: Suspect shot dead by police," BBC News, February 9, 2020, https://www.bbc.com/news/world-latin-america-51439016.
32. Kiratiana, "The Iconic Moment Activist Angela Davis Visited Black Brazilian Women," *Zora*, December 5, 2019, https://zora.medium.com/the-iconic-moment-activist-angela-davis-visited-black-brazilian-women-cadee3cf7207.
33. Ibid.
34. Lu Sudré, "'Where is Justice in Brazil?' housing activist asks after more than 70 days in prison," *Brasil de Fato*, September 10, 2019, https://www.brasildefato.com.br/2019/09/10/where-is-justice-in-brazil-housing-activist-asks-after-more-than-70-days-in-prison.
35. Kiratiana, "The Iconic Moment Activist Angela Davis Visited Black Brazilian Women," *Zora*.
36. Carolyn Zerbe Enns, Lillian Comas Díaz, and Thema Bryant-Davis, "Transnational Feminist Theory and Practice: An Introduction," *Women & Therapy*, 44:1–2, (2021):11–26, https://doi.org/10.1080/02703149.2020.1774997.
37. Ibid.
38. Ibid.
39. Chandra Mohanty, *Feminism without borders: Decolonizing theory, practicing solidarity* (Durham: Duke University Press Books, 2003), 7.
40. Angela Davis, "'I Am Because We Are': A conversation between Francia a Márquez Mina and Angela Davis," interview by Mamyrah Dougé-Prosper, University of California, Sep 7, 2021, video, 57:40. https://www.youtube.com/watch?v=qOLZaA509dI.
41. Francia Márquez, "Afro-Colombian activist Francia Márquez, 2018

Goldman Prize Winner, on Stopping Illegal Gold Mining," interview by Amy Goodman, Democracy Now!, May 21, 2018, video, 35:53. https://www.youtube.com/watch?v=6nvkzYmEZc0.

42. Angela Davis, "'I Am Because We Are': A conversation between Francia a Márquez Mina and Angela Davis," interview by Mamyrah Dougé-Prosper, University of California, Sep 7, 2021, video, 59:20. https://www.youtube.com/watch?v=qOLZaA509dI.

43. Keisha-Khan Y. Perry, "The Groundings with my Sisters: Toward a Black Diasporic Feminist Agenda in the Americas," *The Scholar and Feminist Online*, 7.2 (Spring 2009), https://sfonline.barnard.edu/africana/print_perry.htm.

44. Margaret E. Keck and Kathryn Sikkink, "Transnational advocacy networks in international and regional politics," Blackwell Publishers, (1999), https://courses.washington.edu/pbaf531/KeckSikkink.pdf.

45. "On the Imperative of Transnational Solidarity: A U.S. Black Feminist Statement on the Assassination of Marielle Franco," the *Black Scholar*, March 23, 2018, https://www.theblackscholar.org/on-the-imperative-of-transnational-solidarity-a-u-s-black-feminist-statement-on-the-assassination-of-marielle-franco/#.

46. Patricia Hill Collins, *Black Feminist Thought: Knowledge, Consciousness, and the Politics of Empowerment Second Edition* (New York: Routledge, 2000), 290.

47. Karen Juanita Carrillo, "Afro-Colombian activists receive death threats for organizing," New York Amsterdam, May 16, 2019, https://amsterdamnews.com/news/2019/05/16/afro-colombian-activists-receive-death-threats-org.

48. Desmond Tutu, "Archbishop Desmond Tutu On 'Dignity,'" Amnesty International, October 21, 2010, https://www.amnestyusa.org/archbishop-desmond-tutu-on-dignity/#.

CHAPTER 7: LOVE OF POWER

1. Ashley Crossman, "Power Definitions and Examples in Sociology," ThoughtCo, October 25, 2019, https://www.thoughtco.com/power-p2-3026460.

2. André Berten, "Interview with Michel Foucault by André Berten," Catholic University of Louvain in Belgium (May 2019), https://www.on-tenk.com/fr/documentaires/grands-entretiens/entretien-avec-michel-foucault-par-andre-berten.

3. Colin Koopman, "The power thinker: Why Foucault's work on power is more important than ever," *Aeon*, (accessed on May 17, 2022), https://aeon.co/essays/why-foucaults-work-on-power-is-more-important-than-ever.

4. Michel Foucault, *Discipline & Punish: The Birth of the Prison*, Second Vintage Book Edition (New York: Random House, 1995), 200.

5. Ibid, 203.

6. Ibid, 205.
7. Ibid, 199.
8. Bertrand Russell, *Power: A New Social Analysis* (New York: Routledge, 1938).
9. Ibid.
10. Ibid.
11. Patricia Hill Collins, *Black Feminist Thought: Knowledge, Consciousness, and the Politics of Empowerment Second Edition* (New York: Routledge, 2000), 277.
12. Ibid, 281.
13. Ibid, 287.
14. Ibid.
15. Ibid.
16. Ibid, 284.
17. Ibid, 285.
18. Martin Luther King Jr., *Where do we go from here: Chaos or Community?* (Boston: Beacon Press), 29–30.
19. Ibid, 30.
20. Ibid, 3.
21. Jon Else, *True South: Henry Hampton and "Eyes on the Prize," the Landmark Television Series That Reframed the Civil Rights Movement* (New York: Penguin Random House, 2017), 23–24.
22. Stokely Carmichael, "Eyes on the Prize II: America at the Racial Crossroads 1965–1985," interview by Judy Richardson. Blackside, Inc., November 7, 1988, video 2:32, http://repository.wustl.edu/concern /videos/1g05fg455.
23. Ibid, 6:20.
24. Kwame Ture and Charles V. Hamilton, *Black Power: The Politics of Liberation* (New York: Vintage Books, 1992), 54.
25. Martin Luther King Jr., *Where do we go from here: Chaos or Community?*, 64.
26. Ella Baker, "Speech delivered at the Puerto Rico Solidarity Rally," 1974, video, 0:26.
27. Ella Baker, "The Black Woman in the Civil Rights Struggle, speech given at the Institute of the Black World," Atlanta, Georgia, December 31, 1969, https://awpc.cattcenter.iastate.edu/2019/08/09/the-black-woman -in-the-civil-rights-struggle-1969/.
28. Ibid.
29. Julie Creswell, Kevin Draper, and Sapna Maheshwari, "Nike Nearly Dropped Colin Kaepernick Before Embracing Him," *New York Times*, September 26, 2018, https://www.nytimes.com/2018/09/26/sports/nike -colin-kaepernick.html.
30. Kate Gibson, "Colin Kaepernick is Nike's $6 billion man," *CBS MoneyWatch*, September 21, 2018, https://www.cbsnews.com/news/colin -kaepernick-nike-6-billion-man/.

31. "Everything to Know About Nike's 'You Can't Stop Us' Film," NIKE NEWS, July 20, 2020, https://news.nike.com/news/watch-nike-you-can-t-stop-us-film.

32. "Everything to Know About Nike's 'You Can't Stop Us' Film," NIKE NEWS, July 20, 2020, https://news.nike.com/news/watch-nike-you-can-t-stop-us-film.

33. Ralph Lee Smith, "The South's Pupil Placement Laws: Newest Weapon Against Integration," *Commentary*, October 1990, https://www.commentary.org/articles/ralph-smith/the-souths-pupil-placement-lawsnewest-weapon-against-integration/.

34. Martin Luther King Jr., *Where do we go from here: Chaos or Community?*, 1.

35. Ibid, 11.

36. Ella Baker, "The Black Woman in the Civil Rights Struggle, speech given at the Institute of the Black World."

37. Ibid.

38. Patricia Hill Collins, *Black Feminist Thought: Knowledge, Consciousness, and the Politics of Empowerment Second Edition*, x.

39. Ibid, 274–275.

40. Ibid.

41. Ibid.

42. Denise Lu, Jon Huang, Ashwin Seshagiri, Haeyoun Park, and Troy Griggs, "Faces of Power: 80% Are White, Even as U.S. Becomes More Diverse," *New York Times*, September 9, 2020, https://www.nytimes.com/interactive/2020/09/09/us/powerful-people-race-us.html.

43. The data used for the analysis in this book come from the decennial census for the years 1940 through 2000. For 2010 and 2019, the data source is the American Community Survey (ACS), which included questions on occupation, income, and other characteristics that were previously included in the census for a sample of the population. The ACS for 2019 was used because the COVID pandemic adversely affected the response to the ACS in 2020.

44. Martin Luther King Jr., *Where do we go from here: Chaos or Community?*, 61.

CHAPTER 8: DE NOVO (A NEW BEGINNING)

1. "The Book of Kohelet (Ecclesiastes): Chapter 7, Jewish Virtual Library, Portions Copyright by Benyamin Pilant (1997) and JPS Electronic Edition Copyright by Larry Nelson (1998), https://www.jewishvirtuallibrary.org/kohelet-ecclesiastes-chapter-7.

2. Sarah Bradford, *Harriet, the Moses of Her People* (New York: Printed by J.J. Little & Co., 1901), 25.

3. The data used for the analysis in this book come from the decennial census for the years 1940 through 2000. For 2010 and 2019, the data source is the American Community Survey (ACS), which included

questions on occupation, income, and other characteristics that were previously included in the census for a sample of the population. The ACS for 2019 was used because the COVID pandemic adversely affected the response to the ACS in 2020.

4.   Alisha Gordon, interview by author, New York, March 25, 2022.